The
2 Day a Week Diet
COOKBOOK

Nancy Baggett & Ruth Glick

Photographs by Nancy Baggett
Project Technical Director
Norman Glick

THE 2 DAY A WEEK DIET COOKBOOK

Nancy Baggett and Ruth Glick

Light Street Press

P.O. Box 1233

Columbia, MD 21044-0233

ISBN: 978-0-9906321-0-8

Printed in the United States of America

Sample Recipes from the Book

Contents

INTRODUCTION

For many people, maintaining desired weight or shedding pounds is an ongoing struggle. Parties, dinners with friends, calorie-laden fast-food meals, and endless opportunities for snacking (encouraged by a barrage of advertisements) constantly entice us to eat more than we should. This is certainly true for the two of us. Because we spend a lot of time creating and testing recipes and sitting and writing about food, we definitely understand dieters' challenges and have been waging our own battle of the bulge for years.

But recently we made a lifestyle change that has been a huge help in our never-ending fight against the dreaded "expanding waistline." We started following what's sometimes referred to as the 5-2 or Fast Diet—but which is in fact more accurately described as the 2 Day a Week Diet. It involves eating normal meals five days a week but cutting back to only 500 calories (guys can eat 600 calories) on two nonconsecutive days.

Immediately we began looking for some easy-to-prepare, low-calorie recipes that could both comfortably fit in the 500- or 600-calorie, diet-day budget and that were the kinds of tempting, everyday dishes we enjoy. But, frankly, we were disappointed to discover that very few of the recipes available were as tasty or as doable as we wanted. So, we decided to put our own professional expertise at developing healthy and special-diet recipes to work and devise dishes we *did* like. (Our credits include cookbooks and recipes for many "healthy eating" organizations, including the American Diabetes Association, Rodale Books, *Prevention*, and *Eating Well*.)

Ruth, later joined by Nancy, began creating low-calorie recipes that easily fit her busy schedule *and* that she and her husband really enjoyed as they followed the 2 Day a Week diet together. After Nancy started developing recipes, she and her husband began using the diet, too. Here in *The 2 Day a Week Diet Cookbook* are the 75 kitchen-tested, diet-day dishes we felt were the best ones. Now we are pleased to share them with you.

What's in The *2 Day a Week Diet Cookbook*?

We firmly believe that this book provides everything you need to succeed on the 2 Day a Week Diet. Our 75 carefully crafted recipes are all 200 calories or fewer, so they offer lots of tempting "mix and match" options for how you can spend your 500 or 600 calories and eat well on diet days. The book also includes helpful cooking, and time-saving tips; sample menus; and strategies for fitting the recipes and diet into your lifestyle. Finally, you'll find tips to help you buy the right ingredients (most of which are readily available at your local supermarket), measure them properly, and, ultimately, to turn out the low-calorie dishes that enable you to shed weight.

As you look through our recipes, you'll probably be surprised at how varied and, yes, gratifying 200- or fewer-calorie dishes can be. From breakfast and lunch, through dinner and snacks, you'll find appealing, streamlined versions of old favorites including Home-Style Chicken-Vegetable-Rice Soup, New England Clam Chowder, Microwave "Baked" Apples, and French Toast.

The book also includes many ethnic-inspired options like Guilt Free Chili, shown here, Ginger-Shrimp and Vegetables Skillet, Singapore Noodles with Chicken, and Five-Vegetable Gazpacho. And you'll find some slightly more exotic but equally tempting selections including the Artichoke and Shrimp Salad (pictured below) and Greek-Style Fish Skillet and dishes for vegetarians—like Bean and Cheese Tostadas, Curried Lentil-Vegetable Soup, and Moroccan-Style Winter Squash and Garbanzo Bean Stew.

And, oh yes, the book serves up a number of handy treats including quick Microwave "Grilled" Cheese Sandwich Snack and Mixed Berry Smoothie to help you with those snack attacks.

Finally, we have kept in mind those with a gluten sensitivity. Most dishes are gluten-free, but in cases where we call for a product that contains gluten, we suggest alternatives. Instead of low-carb bread in sandwiches, try substituting rice cakes, corn cakes (thins), gluten-free bagel chips or crackers and serve open-faced. With any of these products, look at the nutritional label and adjust the amount you eat to get the equivalent of the 40-45 calories in a slice of "light" bread. When only bread can be used in a recipe, substitute your favorite gluten-free version. Remember that, because of the higher number of calories, you'll have to cut the amount of bread used. When a recipe calls for low-calorie English muffins, use corn cakes (thins) or rice cakes. Similarly, substitute gluten-free tortillas when tortillas are called for. Again, make calorie adjustments.

The 2 Day a Week Diet Cookbook provides a particularly generous collection of interesting, calorie-wise soups and salads. That's because these can be served in fairly ample 1- to 2-cup servings that fill you up and provide a lot of eating satisfaction—which definitely helps on diet days. (In fact, soups, salads, and snacks may become a mainstay in your regime; they are in ours.)

By the way, it's possible to eat three light meals (that add up to 500 or fewer calories in total) during your diet day, or to choose very-low-calorie recipes and graze every few hours. Or you can make a main dish, eat only half a serving, and save the rest for another mini-meal. (Our sample menus , below, are provided to get you started.)

A Diet That's Remarkably Straightforward and Doable.

For us the best thing about the 2 day a week diet is that it's been easy to stick with—and we've lost weight. Over four months, Ruth has lost 16 pounds and Nancy, who never loses anything on any diet, has lost 5! (Several controlled comparative studies of groups of dieters have shown that our results aren't unique. One study at the University Hospital, South Manchester, England, found that 65 percent of 2-day-diet participants lost weight compared to only 40 percent of those on more typical everyday diet plans.) Of course, you should check with your doctor before starting this or any other diet to make sure it's suitable for you.

The fact that the plan calls for dieting on only two days each week makes it amazingly convenient and easy. We can stick with each diet day better just knowing that we'll be back to eating normally the next day. Perhaps surprisingly, we don't find that we overeat on subsequent non-dieting days either and, in general, are satisfied with less food than before. (Studies have shown this is often true for those who follow the diet.)

Another big advantage of the 2 Day a Week Diet is that it quickly counterbalances the inevitable moments when we overindulge. We know that if we splurge a little at a party or a restaurant, we'll be able to undo any diet damage right away. Plus, since we have the flexibility to select *which* two nonconsecutive diet days in the week are most convenient, we can fit them in and around our travels, vacations, and holiday plans.

So, we hope you're now eager to jump in and get started. Come along on our weight-loss journey. Our trip has been quite slimming (and much easier than we expected), and we hope yours will be too.

CHAPTER 1 – MAKING THE MOST OF THE BOOK

The 2 Day a Week Diet Cookbook gives you everything you need to lose weight and to keep the 2 Day a Week Diet convenient and easy. Instead of tedious meals filled with celery sticks and nonfat cottage cheese, you have a whole array of wonderful dishes that can actually make diet-day dining enjoyable. Here are some approaches we've found helpful as we've been cooking light and dropping those unwanted pounds.

Strategies for shedding the most weight with our recipes.

▶ Always read nutrition labels while shopping, and always use the specific calorie-wise products the recipes call for— like "light" bread and "light" mayo. If you "cheat" and use the regular higher-calorie products, your calories per serving can easily skyrocket to 400 to 500 and sabotage your good intentions and sink your diet ship for the whole day!

▶ Measure ingredients carefully. The only way to ensure that the calorie counts of your dishes match the counts given in the book is to use ingredients in the correct quantities. We usually indicate amounts in cups, so there's no guessing about whether an apple, or zucchini, or onion, or other item is "medium" or "large." (In cases where recipes use an entire package or a labeled product or call for meat, amounts may be specified in ounces.) Don't just "eyeball" quantities because the calories in your dish may be thrown off.

▶ Follow our garnishing guidelines. Throughout the book, we call for lots of garnishes and extras to boost taste and eye appeal and, often, to round out nutrition as well. While some toppers, like chopped parsley and chives, are almost calorie freebies, many, including nuts, seeds, cheese, and olives can quickly turn a calorie-wise dish into a diet disaster. But not to worry; we always give instructions on exactly how much of this or that garnish to use to ensure that you won't inadvertently go awry.

Making the Diet Fit Your Lifestyle

▶ Plan ahead for those really busy diet days. We tell you throughout the book which recipes can be refrigerated or frozen and for how long. By preparing dishes in advance and stashing ready-to-use portions, you'll reduce diet-day stress and have a healthful meal whenever you need it.

▶ Jump-start recipes by using lean-cooked meat, poultry, or seafood left over from "regular" meals. Plain-roasted chicken breast or turkey white meat or leftover shrimp or lean ham, for example, can be the basis of a really tempting and quick diet-day dish, like the Kale, Vegetable, and Ham Stew shown here, particularly if you plan in advance how you'll use them. You may also find it convenient to use deli meats for some recipes. If you do, nitrate-free and reduced-sodium ones are preferred, and look for the lean varieties with 22 calories to 25 calories per ounce.

▶ Cut recipe preparation time by relying on healthful convenience products. Washed and trimmed vegetables, slaw and salad mixes, shredded cheeses, and already-seasoned and diced canned tomatoes are just some of the many great time-savers that we use and that can help you.

▶ Feel free to supplement the recipes in the book with handy, calorie-wise, ready-to-eat purchased treats. Because many of our main dishes and all our side dishes are well under 200 calories a serving, they give you room to fit in welcome little treats such as small servings of strawberries (25 calories per 1/2 cup) or blueberries (41 calories per 1/2 cup), or small cartons of nonfat, low-calorie yogurt, or calorie-controlled packets of light, multigrain crackers and similar nibbles. (Check out, below, our convenient list of healthful items, each containing under 25 calories.)

About the Recipes

Besides limiting calories, our recipes are carefully designed for healthy eating. And so you can see at a glance exactly what you're getting, each recipe has been nutritionally analyzed with professional software and includes a label showing not only the calories, but the fat, sodium, carbohydrates, and protein per serving. Additionally, to help you conveniently and quickly plan your diet day, the calories per serving and portion sizes are also included right at the beginning of each recipe.

Another thing we want you to know: We carefully tested all the recipes—including the ones that aren't pictured in the book. Testing is the only way to make sure that the dishes taste good and the recipes will work for you in your kitchen.

It's important to use the particular ingredients called for and to follow the instructions. In ordinary cooking, there's often some leeway for putting your own spin on a dish. In this case, do make the recipes as written, since they're designed to boost flavor, eating pleasure, and nutrition while also minimizing calories and simplifying preparations.

Occasionally, ingredients, instructions, or techniques may seem unusual, but please stick with them. We think you'll find that they'll deliver the best tasting, most satisfying food with the least amount of effort.

Sample Menus for Tempting Diet-Day Meals

The 2 Day a Week Diet Cookbook provides lots of ways to mix and match recipes to fit within your diet-day calorie limit. To get you started, here are some sample menus that *all* "weigh in" at exactly 500 calories. Remember that guys following this plan get to add another 100 calories to their budget.

Menu 1:
500-Calorie, 3-Meals-a-Day

Breakfast
Ham and Spinach Scramble–110 cal

Lunch
Diet-Day Vegetable Soup–90 cal
Microwave "Grilled" Cheese Sandwich Snack–70 cal

Afternoon Snack
Pomegranate Pop–60 cal

Dinner
Asian-Style Chicken-Apple Salad 170 cal or Greek-Style Fish
Skillet–170 cal

Menu 2:
500-Calorie, 3-Meals-a-Day

Breakfast
French Toast–120 cal topped with Blueberry Sauce–30 cal
(Or substitute purchased low-calorie syrup or low-sugar
blueberry jam)

Lunch
New England Clam Chowder or Manhattan Clam Chowder–
180 cal

Dinner
Bean and Cheese Tostada–120 cal
Ranch Dressing–40 cal over 1 1/2 cups mixed greens–10 cal

Menu 3:
500-Calorie, 3-Meals-a-Day

Breakfast
Mixed Berry Smoothie–110 cal

Lunch
Mock Pizza Omelet–150 cal
Crudités–10 cal and Spinach Dip–30 cal

Supper
Tex-Mex Ground Beef and Vegetable Soup–140 cal
Zesty Coleslaw–60 cal

Menu 4:
500-Calorie, Grazing

Early Morning
Microwave "Baked" Apple–100 cal

Late Morning
Half of Tuna Sandwich–100-cal

Mid Afternoon
Mexican-Style Vegetable Soup–110 cal

Early Evening
Half of Tuna Sandwich–100 cal

Late Evening
Strawberry Lassi–90 cal

Menu 5:
500-Calorie, Vegetarian, 3 Meals a Day

Breakfast
Banana-Chocolate Breakfast Smoothie–170 cal

Lunch
Curried Potato and Cauliflower Soup–120 cal
Russian Dressing–25 cal over 1/2 cup cucumber slices–5 cal

Dinner
Middle Eastern Hummus-Veggie Sandwich Wrap–180 cal

Menu 6:
500-Calorie, Grazing

Early Morning
Sausage Hash–170 cal

Late Morning
Creamy Tomato Soup–70 cal

Mid Afternoon
Microwave "Grilled" Cheese Sandwich Snack–70 cal

Early Evening
"Fried Rice"–110 cal

Late Evening
Banana Pop–90 cal

Menu 7:
500-Calorie, 3 Meals

<u>Breakfast</u>
2 Minute Baked Egg 'n Muffin Breakfast–120 cal

<u>Lunch</u>
Milanese Vegetable Soup–160 cal

<u>Dinner</u>
Beef and Mushroom Pasta Sauce over Spaghetti Squash–190 cal
Marinated Cucumbers, double serving–30 cal

Healthy 1- to 25-Calorie Snacks

On diet days, we like to have low-calorie vegetables and fruits around to snack on, or turn into salads, or serve with low-cal dips. Here's a handy list of some of the lightest, most appealing options. The list can help you fill in gaps when you're aiming for your 500- or 600-calorie daily total.

1 calorie   1 medium radish

2 calories   1 sweet pepper slice

3 calories   1 cauliflower floret

5 calories   1 green onion

6 calories   1 stalk celery (or 6 celery sticks)

7 calories   1 cup spinach

8 calories   1/2 cup cucumber slices

8 calories	1 medium dill pickle
9 calories	1 cup mixed greens
10 calories	1 cup romaine leaves
11 calories	1 broccoli floret
11 calories	1/2 cup sliced fresh mushrooms
13 calories	1/2 cup cherry tomatoes
15 calories	4 carrot sticks or 3 baby carrots
16 calories	1/2 cup chopped kale
17 calories	1 cup shredded cabbage
19 calories	3 cauliflower florets with 1 tablespoon bottled salsa
20 calories	1/3 cup fresh blackberries
20 calories	1/3 cup fresh raspberries
20 calories	1/2 cup watermelon cubes
20 calories	1/2 medium peach
20 calories	1/3 cup diced fresh cantaloupe
20 calories	1 cup of coffee plus 1 tablespoon half and half
21 calories	1/3 cup diced fresh honeydew melon
24 calories	8 medium strawberries

24 calories   2 teaspoons of our Russian Dressing with 3 radishes, 2 cauliflower florets, or 3 celery sticks

25 calories   1/4 cup fresh blueberries

25 calories   1 tablespoon of our Creamy Ranch Dressing with 6 radishes, 1 large cauliflower floret, or 5 celery sticks

25 calories   1 cup shredded lettuce plus 1 tablespoon of our Russian Dressing

Useful Ingredients to Keep on Hand

We call for some ingredients over and over in our recipes. So, you may want to keep the following in stock.

▸ <u>Herbs and spices.</u> These are a super way to add flavor without boosting calories, so recipes in the book often call for them. Here are some you'll find especially useful: thyme, basil, caraway, ginger, and chili powder, and time-saving herb or spice blends including Italian dried herb seasoning and curry powder. (Some of our dishes also get their great taste and aroma from fresh herbs and spices like fresh gingerroot, basil, chives, parsley, and dill, but these, of course, must be purchased as needed.)

▸ <u>Salad greens and other low-cal vegetables.</u> All sorts of lettuces, cabbage, and spinach, plus celery, cauliflower, summer squash, cucumber, mushrooms, and radishes are useful for diet days. The reason: They can add welcome color, texture, nutrients, and volume to many dishes, yet are fairly low-calorie or nearly calorie-free.

- ▶ <u>Low-cal condiments.</u> These can really crank up flavor, yet most add few calories to dishes. Here are ones we suggest you keep on hand: hot pepper sauce, mustard, vinegars, low-calorie salad dressing, bottled salsa, prepared horseradish, soy sauce, chopped garlic, and salt. If you have a gluten sensitivity, be sure to use gluten-free versions.

- ▶ <u>Reduced-fat or light mayonnaise.</u> This is a handy addition to many homemade salad dressings and sandwich fillings. Our recipes always call for mayonnaise that has 35 calories per tablespoon. If you find a lighter version you like, feel free to use it.

- ▶ <u>Reduced-calorie bread</u>. If we call for bread or English muffins in a recipe, we're referring to a reduced-calorie version. Look for "light" or "low-carb" bread with 40 to 45 calories per slice and English muffins with 100 calories per muffin (50 calories per half). If you must avoid gluten, choose whatever gluten-free product you like; then adjust the total calorie count of the recipe as necessary. Currently, very few gluten-free breads come in light or low-cal versions. We specifically suggest options in individual recipes.

▶ Reduced-fat or fat-free dairy products. Many of our recipes, from dressings and dips to smoothies and soups, save calories by using reduced-fat milk and buttermilk, and fat-free half and half, sour cream, and yogurt. And reduced-fat cheese works well in our egg dishes and sandwiches.

▶ Tomatoes and tomato products. Fresh tomatoes and various tomato products turn up frequently in our recipes. Some, including fresh tomatoes, canned tomatoes, salsa, and tomato sauce, are all relatively low in calories. Others, including marinara sauce, pizza sauce, and spaghetti sauce, can vary greatly calorie-wise, so check labels to make sure you are buying ones that have at most 40 to 60 calories per serving. If you are gluten-sensitive, also make sure the brand is wheat-free.

▶ Fat-free broth and bouillon. Many soup and stew recipes start with fat-free broth or bouillon because these add rich taste and satisfying volume but few calories. And they reduce calories and heighten flavor in some dressings and skillet dishes as well. Since these products can vary greatly in calorie content, read labels to make sure you are getting the lightest, leanest versions.

▶ Sweeteners. Actually, relatively few recipes in the book call for sweeteners, and they are used in small quantities. But, if you are aiming to consume the fewest calories possible on diet days, you may want to have an artificial sweetener on hand. We don't specify which one, since you probably have your own favorite. Occasionally, dishes call for a small amount of sugar, but you can substitute a non-sugar sweetener if you wish.

▶ Cornstarch. This is a simple way to thicken while keeping dishes gluten-free, so it turns up to replace flour in several of our recipes.

Now on to the recipes.

CHAPTER 2 – SOUPS

Creamy Tomato Soup

New England Clam Chowder

Manhattan Clam Chowder

Home-Style Chicken-Vegetable-Rice Soup

Diet-Day Vegetable Soup

Lentil Vegetable Soup

Milanese Vegetable Soup

Curried Lentil-Vegetable Soup

Curried Potato and Cauliflower Soup

Tex-Mex Ground Beef and Vegetable Soup

Mexican-Style Vegetable Soup

Mushroom-Spinach-Pasta Soup

Quick Tomato-Pumpkin Bisque

Spiced Pumpkin Soup

Five-Vegetable Gazpacho

Creamy Tomato Soup

This soup is a true marvel, an astonishing 60 calories per serving but surprisingly satisfying and also quick to make. On diet days, we like to pair it with our quick Microwave "Grilled" Cheese Sandwich Snack, The calories for the total meal are still under 200.

Tip: We also like this soup just fine without the half and half. Leaving it out saves 20 calories a serving!

Makes 2 60-calorie servings, about 1 1/4 cups each.

1 1/2 cups fat-free chicken broth or bouillon

1 8-oz can tomato sauce

1/4 cup fat-free half and half

2 to 3 drops hot pepper sauce, optional

Fresh ground black pepper for garnish, optional

1. In a medium-sized nonreactive saucepan, combine broth and tomato sauce. Add half and half, and stir to mix well.

2. Heat over medium heat to piping hot and serve. Garnish with fresh ground black pepper, if desired.

Soup will keep in the refrigerator 2 or 3 days. Or freeze for up to 2 weeks for longer storage. If soup has been refrigerated or frozen, reheat and stir before serving.

Nutrition Facts

Serving Size 1 1/4 cups (322g)
Servings Per Container 2

Amount Per Serving

Calories 60   Calories from Fat 5

	% Daily Value*
Total Fat 0.5g	**1%**
Saturated Fat 0g	**0%**
Trans Fat 0g	
Cholesterol 0mg	**0%**
Sodium 1360mg	**57%**
Total Carbohydrate 10g	**3%**
Dietary Fiber 2g	**8%**
Sugars 7g	
Protein 4g	

New England Clam Chowder

Clams are a wonderful low-cal source of protein. Here they star in a tasty New England chowder that's enhanced with herbs. If you're fond of fresh parsley, you'll probably like it a lot garnishing the chowder. And feel free to add all you want; it's high in vitamins A and C yet very low in calories.

Note that since the soup is thickened with cornstarch, it's gluten free, like almost all of our recipes.

Makes 2 180-calorie servings, about 2 cups each.

1 6.5-oz can minced clams, including juice

1 1/2 cups fat-free chicken broth or bouillon

1 cup cubed red-skin potatoes, peeled or unpeeled

1 cup coarsely chopped cauliflower florets

1/2 cup chopped celery

1/2 tsp *each* dried thyme and basil leaves

1 bay leaf

1/2 cup 2-percent-fat milk

1 Tbsp cornstarch

1/4 cup fat-free half and half

Salt and white pepper to taste

1. Drain clam liquid into large, heavy saucepan or small Dutch oven, reserving clams in a small bowl. To pot, add chicken broth, potatoes, cauliflower, celery, thyme, basil, and bay leaf.

2. Bring to boil, cover, lower heat, and simmer 12 to 16 minutes, until potatoes are very tender when tested with a fork.

3. Meanwhile, in a 2-cup measure, thoroughly stir together milk and cornstarch.

4. Remove bay leaf from pot, and discard. Stir in milk-cornstarch mixture. Bring back to a boil, and cook, stirring frequently, 3 minutes until mixture thickens. Stir in clams and half and half. Lower heat, cover, and simmer 3 to 5 minutes longer until flavors are well blended.

Serve at once or keep in refrigerator for 2 or 3 days. The chowder can be frozen for up to 3 weeks.

Nutrition Facts

Serving Size 2 cups (511g)
Servings Per Container 2

Amount Per Serving

Calories 180   Calories from Fat 15

% Daily Value*

Total Fat 2g	3%
Saturated Fat 1g	5%
Trans Fat 0g	
Cholesterol 20mg	7%
Sodium 1400mg	58%
Total Carbohydrate 27g	9%
Dietary Fiber 3g	12%
Sugars 8g	
Protein 13g	

Manhattan Clam Chowder

Canned clams and fresh vegetables team up to make a hearty main-dish soup. Our slimmed-down version of this classic recipe is low in calories, high in flavor, and convenient to prepare.

Makes 3 180-calorie servings, about 1 2/3 cups each.

1 6.5-oz can minced clams, including juice

2 1/2 cups fat-free chicken broth or bouillon

3/4 cup chopped celery

1/2 cup diced sweet green pepper

1 cup cubed red-skin potatoes, peeled or unpeeled

1 cup chopped green cabbage

1 tsp Italian dried herb seasoning

1 15.2-oz can tomato sauce

2 to 3 drops hot pepper sauce, or to taste

Salt to taste

1. Drain clam liquid into a large, heavy saucepan or small Dutch oven, reserving the clams in a small bowl. To the pot, add chicken broth, celery, green pepper, potatoes, cabbage, and Italian seasoning.

2. Bring to a boil, cover, lower heat, and simmer 12 to 16 minutes, until potatoes are very tender when tested with a fork.

3. Add clams, tomato sauce, and hot pepper sauce. Bring to a boil. Lower heat, cover, and simmer about 5 minutes longer until flavors are well blended.

Serve at once or keep in refrigerator for 2 or 3 days. The chowder can be frozen for up to 3 weeks.

Nutrition Facts

Serving Size 1 2/3 (784g)
Servings Per Container 3

Amount Per Serving

Calories 180   Calories from Fat 5

% Daily Value*

Total Fat 0.5g	**1%**
Saturated Fat 0g	**0%**
Trans Fat 0g	
Cholesterol 15mg	**5%**
Sodium 2880mg	**120%**
Total Carbohydrate 31g	**10%**
Dietary Fiber 5g	**20%**
Sugars 6g	
Protein 15g	

Home-Style Chicken-Vegetable-Rice Soup

It's easy to turn roasted chicken white meat left over from a "regular" meal into appealing diet-day "comfort food" fare. You can make this recipe using leftover turkey breast meat in place of chicken; in this case, the soup servings will have 140 calories each.

To enrich the flavor of the broth a bit, we simmer it with some thyme, parsley, and green onion tops while we ready the rest of the ingredients. It's a small step, but it makes the soup seem a little more full-bodied—a very good thing on a diet day.

Tip: If you don't have fresh thyme or parsley sprigs, substitute 3/4 teaspoon of dried thyme leaves. Don't bother substituting for the fresh parsley; the dried doesn't have much taste.

Makes 4 130-calorie servings, about 1 2/3 cups each.

8 cups fat-free, reduced-sodium chicken broth

6 to 7 6-inch thyme sprigs and parsley sprigs

1/2 cup chopped green-onion white parts and whole-green tops reserved separately

Scant 1/8 tsp fresh ground black pepper, or to taste

1/4 cup raw long-grain white rice

3/4 cup *each* diced celery and diced cauliflower

1/2 cup thinly sliced carrots

1 cup diced chicken white meat

1/4 tsp salt, optional

1. In a soup pot or very large saucepan, combine broth, thyme and parsley sprigs (or 3/4 teaspoon dried thyme), green onion tops, and black pepper. (Reserve white parts of onions for adding later.) Bring pot to a boil over medium-high heat, then adjust heat so mixture boils gently; cook, uncovered, 10 to 15 minutes while other ingredients are readied.

2. With a slotted spoon, scoop and remove thyme and parsley sprigs (if using) and green onion tops from pot and discard. Stir onion white parts, rice, celery, cauliflower, and carrots into pot. Bring mixture to a gentle boil, and cook, covered, for 10 minutes.

3. Add chicken to pot and continue cooking, covered, until rice and carrots are tender, about 10 minutes longer. Taste and add salt, if desired. Serve immediately or cover and refrigerate for later use.

Soup keeps, refrigerated, for up to 4 days, and frozen, airtight, for up to 1 month.

Nutrition Facts

Serving Size 1 2/3 cups (525g)
Servings Per Container 4

Amount Per Serving

Calories 130   Calories from Fat 10

                                                          % Daily Value*

Total Fat 1g	**2%**
Saturated Fat 0.5g	**3%**
Trans Fat 0g	
Cholesterol 25mg	**8%**
Sodium 860mg	**36%**
Total Carbohydrate 16g	**5%**
Dietary Fiber 3g	**12%**
Sugars 3g	
Protein 17g	

Diet-Day Vegetable Soup

This is a wonderful soup for diet days. It's tasty, filling, low in calories, and easy to make. Also, you can vary the vegetables. If you don't have zucchini, for example, you can use more of any of the other vegetables called for in this recipe. We like to make a big batch and keep it in the refrigerator for several days.

Makes 6 90-calorie servings, about 2 cups each.

8 cups fat-free chicken broth or bouillon or vegetable broth

2 cups green beans, trimmed and broken in half

1 cup sliced celery

3 cups thinly sliced green cabbage

2 cups *each* broccoli and cauliflower florets

1 cup large zucchini cubes

1/2 cup coarsely chopped parsley leaves

1 tsp *each* dried thyme leaves and basil leaves

1 bay leaf

1 cup canned diced tomatoes, including juice

1. Place broth in a large pot, and bring to a gentle boil. Add green beans and celery.

2. Once liquid is boiling, add cabbage, broccoli, cauliflower, zucchini, and parsley. Then add thyme, basil, and bay leaf.

3. Reduce heat, cover, and simmer for about 15 minutes until green beans are tender when tested with a fork.

4. Add tomatoes and simmer an additional 10 to 15 minutes until vegetables are tender when pierced with a fork. Remove bay leaf before serving.

The soup will keep for 3 or 4 days in the refrigerator and can be frozen for up to 2 weeks for longer storage.

Nutrition Facts

Serving Size 2 cups (547g)
Servings Per Container 6

Amount Per Serving

Calories 90   Calories from Fat 5

	% Daily Value*
Total Fat 0g	**0%**
Saturated Fat 0g	**0%**
Trans Fat 0g	
Cholesterol 0mg	**0%**
Sodium 710mg	**30%**
Total Carbohydrate 12g	**4%**
Dietary Fiber 5g	**20%**
Sugars 6g	
Protein 12g	

Lentil Vegetable Soup

This is a nice variation on the vegetable soup theme. Lentils boost protein, give the soup texture and flavor, and help thicken the broth. To add robust taste without a lot of fuss, the recipe calls for marinara sauce.

Tip: Check labels, and be sure to use a marinara sauce that has 45 calories or fewer per 1/2 cup. For a slightly different taste, if you like, you can substitute salsa with the same number of calories for marinara sauce.

This is one of those soups that you can make in large quantities and store in the refrigerator or freezer for second and third helpings.

Makes 4 150-calorie servings, about 2 cups each.

1/4 cup dry green lentils, washed and picked over

6 cups fat-free chicken broth or bouillon or vegetable broth

2 cups thinly sliced green cabbage

2 cups small cauliflower florets

1/2 cup frozen corn kernels

1/2 cup sliced celery

1 bay leaf

1 tsp Italian dried herb seasoning

1 cup marinara sauce

Salt and pepper to taste, optional

1. Combine lentils and broth in a medium-sized pot. Bring to a boil and reduce heat to a simmer.

2. Add cabbage, cauliflower, corn, celery, bay leaf, and Italian seasoning. Return to a boil, reduce heat, cover, and cook at a low boil for 30 to 35 minutes or until lentils are tender.

3. Stir in marinara sauce, remove bay leaf; and reheat to piping hot. Add salt and pepper, if desired.

The soup will keep for 3 or 4 days in the refrigerator and can be frozen for up to 2 weeks for longer storage.

Nutrition Facts

Serving Size 2 cups (543g)
Servings Per Container 4

Amount Per Serving

Calories 150	Calories from Fat 20

	% Daily Value*
Total Fat 2.5g	4%
Saturated Fat 0g	0%
Trans Fat 0g	
Cholesterol 0mg	0%
Sodium 1700mg	71%
Total Carbohydrate 25g	8%
Dietary Fiber 7g	28%
Sugars 8g	
Protein 8g	

Milanese Vegetable Soup

Soup is a great way to fill yourself up on a diet day, especially if you can make it quickly and conveniently. As you can see from the directions, there's almost nothing to making this flavorful, chunky lunch or dinner entrée. Because there's no meat to add calories, we've indulged ourselves by adding chickpeas because we love their taste and texture. But if you prefer, you could leave them out and save 50 calories per serving.

Makes 2 160-calorie servings, about 2 1/4 cups each.

1 1/2 cups canned diced tomatoes, including juice

4 cups fat-free chicken broth or bouillon or vegetable broth

1 1/2 cups diced zucchini

1 1/2 cups small cauliflower florets

1/2 cup coarsely chopped parsley leaves

1/2 cup canned chickpeas, well drained

1 tsp Italian dried herb seasoning blend

1. Combine tomatoes, broth, zucchini, cauliflower, parsley, chickpeas, and Italian seasoning in a large saucepan or medium-sized pot. Bring to a boil.

2. Reduce heat and simmer, covered, 10 to 12 minutes, until zucchini and cauliflower are tender.

Soup will keep, covered, in refrigerator for 3 or 4 days. Or freeze, airtight, for up to 1 month.

Nutrition Facts

Serving Size 2 1/4 cups (930g)
Servings Per Container 2

Amount Per Serving

Calories 160   Calories from Fat 20

	% Daily Value*
Total Fat 2g	3%
Saturated Fat 0g	0%
Trans Fat 0g	
Cholesterol 0mg	0%
Sodium 2450mg	102%
Total Carbohydrate 27g	9%
Dietary Fiber 9g	36%
Sugars 10g	
Protein 10g	

Curried Lentil-Vegetable Soup

Full of zesty flavor and high in fiber from brown rice and red lentils, this soup is very healthful, without tasting even slightly "health-foody." It's also quite economical. Depending on the curry powder used, the soup can be slightly spicy or pack a good bit of heat.

Makes 4 160-calorie servings, about 1 2/3 cups each.

1 1/2 tsp olive oil

3/4 cup *each* coarsely chopped onion and chopped celery

1/2 cup *each* chopped sweet red or green pepper and diced carrots

6 cups fat-free reduced-sodium chicken broth or vegetable broth

1/4 cup *each* uncooked red lentils and uncooked long-grain brown rice

2 to 3 tsp mild to medium-hot curry powder (your preference)

1 tsp dried thyme leaves

3/4 tsp ground cardamom *or* 1 tsp ground allspice

1 14.5-oz can diced tomatoes (or tomatoes seasoned with garlic and oregano), including juice

1/4 tsp *each* salt and black pepper, or to taste

2 Tbsp chopped cilantro leaves for garnish, optional

1. Combine oil, onion, celery, sweet pepper, and carrots in a 4-quart soup pot or saucepan. Cook over medium heat, stirring constantly, until they are soft and beginning to brown, about 5 minutes.

2. Add broth, lentils, rice, curry powder, thyme, and cardamom to pot. Bring to a boil over medium heat, stirring frequently. Adjust heat so the mixture just barely simmers; cover and cook, stirring occasionally, until rice is just tender, about 20 to 25 minutes.

3. Stir in tomatoes and their juice. Bring back to a boil. Add salt and pepper to taste. Serve in soup plates, garnished with fresh cilantro, if desired.

Keeps, covered and refrigerated, for up to 4 days. May be frozen for up to 2 weeks.

Nutrition Facts

Serving Size 1 2/3 cups (522g)
Servings Per Container 4

Amount Per Serving

Calories 160   Calories from Fat 25

% Daily Value*

Total Fat 2.5g	**4%**
Saturated Fat 0g	**0%**
Trans Fat 0g	
Cholesterol 0mg	**0%**
Sodium 1090mg	**45%**
Total Carbohydrate 28g	**9%**
Dietary Fiber 6g	**24%**
Sugars 6g	
Protein 8g	

Curried Potato and Cauliflower Soup

Remarkably thick, creamy, and full-bodied, this curried soup makes a wonderful change of pace from more traditional recipes.

Tip: An immersion blender makes preparation easy, but you can also transfer the soup in batches to a food processor for pureeing. If using an immersion blender, make sure the pot is large enough to prevent splashing. We like to leave some pieces of cauliflower and potato in the soup; but if you prefer a completely smooth texture, puree it completely. Also, do not overcook the milk and cornstarch mixture as it could overflow the measuring cup.

Makes 2 120-calorie servings, about 1 1/2 cups each.

3 cups small cauliflower florets

2 cups fat-free chicken broth or bouillon or vegetable broth

1 cup peeled potato cubes

1/2 tsp minced garlic

1 tsp *each* mild curry powder and ground cumin

1/2 cup 2-percent-fat milk

1 Tbsp cornstarch

Salt and white pepper to taste

1. In a large saucepan or small Dutch oven, combine cauliflower, broth, potato, garlic, curry powder, and cumin.

Bring to a boil, then reduce heat. Cover, and boil gently for 10 to 12 minutes or until cauliflower and potato are tender when tested with a fork.

2. Remove pot from heat. With an immersion blender, puree cauliflower and potato, leaving some larger pieces, if desired. Alternatively, transfer in batches to a food processor, and process to desired consistency. If a food processor is used, return soup to pot.

3. In a 2-cup measure, thoroughly stir together milk and cornstarch. Cover with wax paper, and microwave on high power 1 minute, or until mixture has thickened; watch carefully.

4. Using the immersion blender, thoroughly blend the milk mixture into the soup. Return to burner, and heat to piping hot. Add salt and pepper to taste.

Soup will keep in refrigerator, covered, 1 or 2 days.

Nutrition Facts

Serving Size 1 1/2 cups (469g)
Servings Per Container 2

Amount Per Serving

Calories 120   Calories from Fat 20

% Daily Value*

Total Fat 2g	**3%**
Saturated Fat 1g	**5%**
Trans Fat 0g	
Cholesterol 5mg	**2%**
Sodium 470mg	**20%**
Total Carbohydrate 16g	**5%**
Dietary Fiber 4g	**16%**
Sugars 6g	
Protein 11g	

Tex-Mex Ground Beef and Vegetable Soup

Think of this hearty ground beef and bean soup as a cross between chili and mixed vegetable soup. It makes a hearty lunch or dinner entrée. For extra zip, top each serving with a little more salsa and a few fresh cilantro sprigs.

Makes 4 140-calorie servings, about 2 1/4 cups each.

4 oz extra-lean ground beef

6 cups fat-free beef broth or bouillon

1 cup mild bottled salsa

2 cups coarsely shredded green cabbage

1 cup chopped sweet green pepper

1/2 cup kidney beans

3/4 cup frozen corn kernels

1/2 tsp *each* chili powder and ground cumin, or to taste

1. In a medium-sized pot over medium-high heat, cook ground beef, stirring constantly until lightly browned all over, about 6 minutes. If it begins to stick to the pan, stir in a little broth.

2. Add broth and salsa, then vegetables and seasonings.

3. Cook at a low boil, covered, for 20 to 25 minutes until flavors are well blended and soup has cooked down slightly.

Soup will keep refrigerated for 2 or 3 days. Or freeze for up to 3 weeks.

Nutrition Facts

Serving Size 2 1/4 cups (565g)
Servings Per Container 4

Amount Per Serving

Calories 140   Calories from Fat 20

% Daily Value*

Total Fat 2.5g	**4%**
Saturated Fat 0g	**0%**
Trans Fat 0g	
Cholesterol 15mg	**5%**
Sodium 1770mg	**74%**
Total Carbohydrate 22g	**7%**
Dietary Fiber 4g	**16%**
Sugars 6g	
Protein 11g	

Mexican-Style Vegetable Soup

Surprisingly hearty, this soup makes a perfect lunch or dinner entrée. Bottled salsa gives it a full, rich flavor.

Makes 4 110-calorie servings, about 2 cups each.

4 cups fat-free chicken broth or bouillon or vegetable broth

1 cup mild bottled salsa

2 cups coarsely shredded green cabbage

1 cup chopped sweet red or green pepper

1/2 cup kidney beans

1 cup frozen corn kernels

1/2 tsp *each* chili powder and ground cumin

1. In a medium-sized pot, combine broth and salsa. Add cabbage, sweet pepper, beans, corn, chili powder, and cumin.

2. Bring to a boil. Reduce heat, cover, and simmer for 20 to 25 minutes until soup cooks down slightly and flavors are well blended.

Soup will keep in the refrigerator, covered, for 3 or 4 days. Or freeze, airtight, for up to 3 weeks.

Nutrition Facts

Serving Size 2 cups (431g)
Servings Per Container 4

Amount Per Serving

Calories 110   Calories from Fat 10

	% Daily Value*
Total Fat 1g	**2%**
Saturated Fat 0g	**0%**
Trans Fat 0g	
Cholesterol 0mg	**0%**
Sodium 1390mg	**58%**
Total Carbohydrate 21g	**7%**
Dietary Fiber 4g	**16%**
Sugars 6g	
Protein 7g	

Mushroom-Spinach-Pasta Soup

This soup is admittedly a bit plain looking, and the recipe may seem too simple to be tasty, but in fact it is aromatic and flavorful and makes a light, pleasant diet-day lunch. It's good made with either vegetable or chicken broth, so it can fit into a vegetarian meal. While fresh basil delivers the best results, the dried herb will do nicely.

Tip: For a gluten-free version that can be made exactly the same way, simply substitute 2 1/2 tablespoons "instant" brown rice for the pasta. The calorie count will be the same.

Makes 4 120-calorie servings, about 1 1/4 cups each.

1 Tbsp olive oil

2 1/2 cups sliced mushrooms

1 small garlic clove, peeled and finely chopped

6 cups canned vegetable broth or fat-free reduced-sodium chicken broth

1/4 cup 1-inch pieces regular or multigrain vermicelli, spaghetti, or other thin pasta

3 Tbsp chopped fresh basil leaves or 2 tsp dried basil leaves

1 Tbsp chopped chives or green onions

4 cups (lightly packed) chopped fresh spinach leaves

2 Tbsp shredded or grated Parmesan cheese

Salt and freshly ground black pepper, to taste

1. In a 4-quart saucepan or similar-size soup pot, combine oil and mushrooms. Cook over medium heat, stirring constantly, 6 to 7 minutes or until mushrooms are nicely browned.

2. Add garlic and cook, stirring, 1 minute longer. Stir broth, pasta, and basil, and bring to a boil over high heat. Adjust heat so mixture boils gently, and cook, covered, stirring occasionally, for 4 to 7 minutes or until pasta is almost tender. (Multigrain will take considerably longer than regular pasta.)

3. Stir in spinach and cook, uncovered, until just tender, 2 to 3 minutes longer. Taste and add salt and pepper if desired. Serve immediately, garnished with Parmesan and fresh basil sprigs, if available. Or refrigerate for later use.

Soup will keep refrigerated for up to 3 days and frozen for up to 3 weeks.

Nutrition Facts

Serving Size 1 1/4 cup (399g)
Servings Per Container 4

Amount Per Serving

Calories 120	Calories from Fat 40

	% Daily Value*
Total Fat 4.5g	**7**%
Saturated Fat 1g	**5**%
Trans Fat 0g	
Cholesterol 0mg	**0**%
Sodium 950mg	**40**%
Total Carbohydrate 17g	**6**%
Dietary Fiber 1g	**4**%
Sugars 7g	
Protein 4g	

Quick Tomato-Pumpkin Bisque

You'll notice that this simple, surprisingly hearty bisque contains an unusual ingredient, peanut butter. Yes, it may sound a bit odd, but don't leave it out. Most people don't detect its presence, but it provides protein and lends richness, body, and an underlying satisfying earthiness. For a vegetarian version, simply use vegetable broth instead of chicken broth.

Makes 3 170-calorie servings, about 1 1/4 cups each.

1 15-oz can solid-pack pumpkin (not seasoned pumpkin-pie filling)

About 1 2/3 cups fat-free, reduced-sodium chicken broth or vegetable broth, divided

1 tsp ground allspice

1/2 tsp ground cardamom (substitute 1/4 tsp ground ginger, if necessary)

1/8 to 1/4 tsp ground cayenne pepper, to taste, optional

1 14 1/2-oz can diced tomatoes (preferably seasoned with garlic, basil, and oregano)

2 1/2 Tbsp reduced-fat smooth peanut butter

3 tsp toasted pumpkin seeds for garnish, optional

1. Combine pumpkin, 1 1/2 cups broth, allspice, cardamom, and cayenne (if using) in a 4-quart pot or saucepan. Bring to a boil over medium-high heat, and boil gently, uncovered, for about 5 minutes to allow flavors to mingle.

2. Meanwhile, combine tomatoes and peanut butter in a food processor. Process until very smooth, at least 3 minutes. Stop and scrape down sides halfway through, and don't under-process.

3. Stir processed mixture back into pot. As necessary, thin bisque with more broth to desired consistency. Taste and add black pepper, if desired. Heat to piping hot, and serve. Garnish each serving with 1 teaspoon pumpkin seeds, if desired.

Soup keeps covered and refrigerated for up to 4 days.

Nutrition Facts

Serving Size 1 1/4 cups (409g)
Servings Per Container 3

Amount Per Serving

Calories 170   Calories from Fat 50

% Daily Value*

Total Fat 5g	**8%**
Saturated Fat 1.5g	**8%**
Trans Fat 0g	
Cholesterol 0mg	**0%**
Sodium 990mg	**41%**
Total Carbohydrate 25g	**8%**
Dietary Fiber 7g	**28%**
Sugars 10g	
Protein 6g	

Spiced Pumpkin Soup

Mention pumpkin and most people think of pumpkin pie at Thanksgiving or jack-o'-lanterns at Halloween. But you can make some excellent savory dishes with pumpkin, including this extra-quick soup, which is just the thing to spice up a fall or winter day. Canned pumpkin speeds the preparation, and fat-free half and half adds richness without a lot of calories.

Tip: Be sure you buy solid-pack canned pumpkin and not pie filling.

Makes 3 110-calorie servings, about 1 1/4 cups each.

1/2 cup chopped onion

1/2 cup chopped celery

1/2 cup shredded or chopped carrot

2 cups fat-free chicken broth or bouillon or vegetable broth, divided

1 cup solid-pack canned pumpkin (not pie filling)

1/8 tsp *each* ground ginger, cinnamon and allspice

Dash ground black pepper

1/4 cup fat-free half and half

1. In a small, microwave-safe bowl, combine onion, celery, carrot, and 1/2 cup of broth. Cover with wax paper, and microwave on high power 3 or 4 minutes, stirring once, until vegetables are tender when tested with a fork.

2. Meanwhile, combine remaining broth, pumpkin, ginger, cinnamon, allspice, and black pepper in a medium-sized saucepan, and stir until smooth. Add microwaved vegetables.

3. Bring to a boil. Lower heat and simmer, covered, about 2 or 3 minutes or until flavors are blended. Stir in half and half, and cook an additional minute, stirring.

Soup keeps covered and refrigerated for up to 4 days.

Nutrition Facts

Serving Size 1 1/4 cups (472g)
Servings Per Container 3

Amount Per Serving

Calories 110   Calories from Fat 10

% Daily Value*

Total Fat 1g	**2%**
Saturated Fat 0g	**0%**
Trans Fat 0g	
Cholesterol 0mg	**0%**
Sodium 740mg	**31%**
Total Carbohydrate 20g	**7%**
Dietary Fiber 5g	**20%**
Sugars 9g	
Protein 9g	

Five-Vegetable Gazpacho

*Fresh tomatoes are the star in this lively, healthful gazpacho, but four other vegetables play a role, too. Fortunately they are **all** low in calories, so we often enjoy this irresistible soup on our diet days. The recipe is always good, but it's sublime when bright, bold-tasting, true vine-ripened summer tomatoes are used.*

Makes 4 100-calorie servings, about 1 cup each.

2 1/2 cups very coarsely chopped fully ripe tomatoes

1/2 cup *each* coarsely diced celery, sweet red pepper, and (peeled) cucumber

2 Tbsp chopped green onion white parts

2 Tbsp red wine vinegar

1 1/2 Tbsp extra-virgin olive oil

Generous 1/4 tsp dried oregano leaves

Generous 1/4 tsp salt, or to taste

1/8 tsp freshly ground black pepper, or to taste

1 1/2 cups bottled or canned tomato juice

Celery sticks, cucumber slices, and sweet red pepper strips for garnish, optional

1. Combine coarsely chopped tomatoes, celery, sweet red pepper, cucumber, green onions, vinegar, olive oil, oregano, salt, and pepper in a food processor. Pulse ingredients until they are finely chopped but not pureed.

2. Turn out mixture into a large nonreactive storage container. Stir in tomato juice. Cover and refrigerate until flavors are well blended and soup is chilled, at least 1 hour and up to 24 hours, if desired. Taste and add more salt and pepper if needed.

3. To serve, ladle soup into stemmed dishes or bowls. Garnish with celery sticks, cucumber slices, and sweet red pepper strips, if desired.

Soup keeps, covered and refrigerated, up to 3 days.

Nutrition Facts

Serving Size 1 cup (247g)
Servings Per Container 4

Amount Per Serving

Calories 100   Calories from Fat 50

% Daily Value*

Total Fat 6g	**9%**
Saturated Fat 1g	**5%**
Trans Fat 0g	
Cholesterol 0mg	**0%**
Sodium 410mg	**17%**
Total Carbohydrate 10g	**3%**
Dietary Fiber 2g	**8%**
Sugars 6g	
Protein 2g	

CHAPTER 3 – SALADS

Turkey and Crunchy Vegetable Chopped Salad

Chopped Salad with Turkey and Blue Cheese

Asian-Style Chicken-Apple Salad

Canadian Bacon, Lettuce, and Tomato Salad

Artichoke and Shrimp Salad

Fiesta Chopped Salad

Turkish Vegetable Salad

Zippy Apple Chopped Salad

Potato Cauliflower Salad

Cauliflower "Couscous" Salad

Spicy Eggplant-Lentil Salad

Zesty Coleslaw

Tomatoes Oregano

Marinated Cucumbers

Turkey and Crunchy Vegetable Chopped Salad

We really enjoy sitting down to this dish. The portions are generous and full of flavor, and the salad is pleasingly crisp. All the crunching and munching somehow makes it seem like we've eaten an extremely satisfying meal—a good feeling on a diet day! Though this recipe calls for leftover roasted turkey breast, you can certainly substitute roaster-chicken white meat if that's what you have on hand.

Tip: For a little extra color and "munchability," feel free to add in a tablespoon of chopped radish or red cabbage when tossing the salad.

Makes 2 180-calorie servings, about 2 1/3 cups each.

1 Tbsp *each* fresh lemon juice and unseasoned rice vinegar

1 Tbsp *each* corn oil or safflower oil and chopped chives or green onions

1 1/2 tsp Dijon-style grainy mustard

1/2 tsp honey

1/8 tsp *each* salt and pepper

3/4 cup cubed (1/2-inch pieces) roasted turkey breast meat

1/3 cup *each* chopped celery and carrot

2 1/2 cups chopped green cabbage

1 1/2 cups chopped romaine or iceberg lettuce

8 cherry tomatoes, halved

1. In a large, nonreactive bowl, stir together lemon juice, vinegar, oil, chives, mustard, honey, salt, and pepper until thoroughly blended. Stir in turkey; let stand while vegetables are readied.

2. Add the celery, carrot, cabbage, and lettuce to bowl. Toss until vegetables are coated. Add tomatoes and serve.

Salad keeps, covered and refrigerated, for up to 24 hours.

Nutrition Facts

Serving Size 2 1/3 cups (221g)
Servings Per Container 2

Amount Per Serving

Calories 180   Calories from Fat 70

% Daily Value*

Total Fat 8g	**12%**
Saturated Fat 0.5g	**3%**
Trans Fat 0g	
Cholesterol 45mg	**15%**
Sodium 310mg	**13%**
Total Carbohydrate 10g	**3%**
Dietary Fiber 3g	**12%**
Sugars 3g	
Protein 19g	

Chopped Salad with Turkey and Blue Cheese

Chopped salads are a mainstay of our diet-day meals because the combination of chunky ingredients gives us a lot of taste and texture in every bite. Some of these salads are made with all vegetables; but others, like this one, might feature meat and/or cheese. Here we've added turkey breast and blue cheese to the greens. Because of its distinct flavor, a little blue cheese goes a long way.

Makes 3 140-calorie servings, about 1 2/3 cups each

1 1/2 Tbsp olive oil

1/2 tsp cider vinegar

1/4 tsp celery salt

3 cups very thinly sliced romaine lettuce, cut crosswise

1 cup *each* small cubes of tomato and cucumber (peeled)

1 cup chopped broccoli (parboiled if desired)

1/2 cup chopped sweet red, yellow or orange pepper

1/4 cup chopped red cabbage

2 oz chopped turkey breast

1 Tbsp crumbled blue cheese

1.In a large bowl, stir together olive oil, vinegar and celery salt.

2.Stir in lettuce, and mix well. Stir in remaining vegetables, then turkey and cheese. Refrigerate for a half hour and up to three hours to allow flavors to blend.

Salad will keep in the refrigerator for 1 or 2 days.

Nutrition Facts

Serving Size 1 2/3 cups (239g)
Servings Per Container 3

Amount Per Serving

Calories 140   Calories from Fat 80

	% Daily Value*
Total Fat 9g	**14%**
Saturated Fat 0.5g	**3%**
Trans Fat 0g	
Cholesterol 10mg	**3%**
Sodium 310mg	**13%**
Total Carbohydrate 10g	**3%**
Dietary Fiber 3g	**12%**
Sugars 5g	
Protein 6g	

Asian-Style Chicken-Apple Salad

This recipe calls for a bag of "Asian" slaw mix, a colorful, healthful, convenience product that makes preparations go quickly. (If your supermarket doesn't happen to carry it, regular cabbage-slaw mix can be substituted.) For best taste and texture choose a very crisp, flavorful, sweet-tart variety of apple. We especially like Honeycrisp, Braeburn, and Golden Delicious.

Note that the salad is dressed with our Ginger-Honey Vinaigrette Dressing. It keeps well, so we like to make it ahead and have it on hand to brighten up steamed broccoli or cabbage, as well as to toss with this salad.

Makes 3 170-calorie servings, about 1 1/3 cups each.

1 12-oz bag ready-to-use Asian slaw mix

2/3 cup diced unpeeled crisp, flavorful apple, plus 9 fresh apple slices for garnish

1/4 cup *each* finely diced celery and green onions, including tender tops

4 oz shredded or diced roasted chicken white meat

1/4 cup Ginger-Honey Vinaigrette Dressing

1 Tbsp sesame seeds, preferably toasted,* for garnish

1. In a large nonreactive bowl stir together slaw mix, diced apple, celery, green onions, and chicken.

2. Stir in vinaigrette, tossing until ingredients are well combined. Garnish with sesame seeds and apple slices just before serving.

Serve immediately or cover and refrigerate for up to 2 days.

*Toasting sesame seeds is optional but brings out their nutty flavor and crunchiness. To toast, simply spread a few tablespoons hulled sesame seeds in a small nonstick skillet over medium heat. Cook, stirring and watching carefully for signs of scorching, for 3 to 5 minutes, or until they are just tinged with brown and very fragrant. If they begin to darken, immediately remove skillet from burner and turn out seeds onto a heat-proof plate until cooled. Store, airtight and refrigerated, for up to 3 months, using as needed.

Nutrition Facts

Serving Size 1 1/3 cups (186g)
Servings Per Container 3

Amount Per Serving

Calories 170   Calories from Fat 80

% Daily Value*

Total Fat 9g   **14%**

   Saturated Fat 1.5g   **8%**

   Trans Fat 0g

Cholesterol 0mg   **0%**

Sodium 190mg   **8%**

Total Carbohydrate 19g   **6%**

   Dietary Fiber 3g   **12%**

   Sugars 6g

Protein 6g

Canadian Bacon, Lettuce, and Tomato Salad

When we first had a version of this salad at an upscale restaurant, we were surprised to find that it included blue-cheese crumbles. The cheese is a nice addition to the dish and adds less than 30 calories per serving. If you have calories to spare for the day, you could include another ounce of bacon in the recipe and only add about 22 calories a serving.

Makes 2 170-calorie servings, about 2 cups each.

2 oz (about 3 slices) Canadian bacon, cut into thin strips

1 Tbsp extra-virgin olive oil

1/4 tsp apple cider vinegar

Salt and black pepper to taste

4 cups torn romaine lettuce

1 cup tomato cubes

2 Tbsp crumbled blue cheese

1. Cook Canadian bacon according to package directions. Set aside.

2. In a large bowl, stir together oil and vinegar. Add salt and pepper to taste. Add lettuce, and stir to coat leaves.

3. Add tomato and bacon, and stir to mix well. Stir in cheese. Serve immediately.

Salad will keep, covered and refrigerated, 1 or 2 days.

Nutrition Facts

Serving Size 2 cups (237g)
Servings Per Container 2

Amount Per Serving

Calories 170   Calories from Fat 110

	% Daily Value*
Total Fat 12g	18%
Saturated Fat 3g	15%
Trans Fat 0g	
Cholesterol 20mg	7%
Sodium 380mg	16%
Total Carbohydrate 9g	3%
Dietary Fiber 2g	8%
Sugars 4g	
Protein 9g	

Artichoke and Shrimp Salad

We like using high-flavor, low-calorie ingredients such as artichokes to enhance the taste of our dishes. Here they perfectly complement the shrimp in this unusual, very tempting salad.

Makes 3 150-calorie servings, about 2/3 cup each.

1/4 cup fat-free dairy sour cream

3 Tbsp light mayonnaise

2 tsp balsamic vinegar

1/2 tsp Italian dried herb seasoning

Dash white pepper

1 cup canned artichoke-heart quarters, any coarse outer leaves discarded

3/4 cup cooked small shrimp

Lettuce leaves for garnish, optional

1. In a small bowl, stir together sour cream, mayonnaise, vinegar, Italian seasoning, and pepper. Stir to mix well. Stir in artichokes and shrimp.

2. Cover and refrigerate at least 1/2 hour and up to 12 hours to allow flavors to blend. Serve on a lettuce leaves, if desired.

Salad will keep, covered, in the refrigerator 1 to 2 days.

Nutrition Facts

Serving Size 2/3 cup (182g)
Servings Per Container 3

Amount Per Serving

Calories 150   Calories from Fat 45

	% Daily Value*
Total Fat 5g	**8%**
Saturated Fat 1g	**5%**
Trans Fat 0g	
Cholesterol 120mg	**40%**
Sodium 1040mg	**43%**
Total Carbohydrate 11g	**4%**
Dietary Fiber 1g	**4%**
Sugars 3g	
Protein 13g	

Fiesta Chopped Salad

Colorful and zesty, this makes a generous and pleasing diet-day lunch. One secret to the flavor is the brine from the black olives, so don't leave it out.

Tip: The heat level of green chiles can vary considerably, so taste them before adding in the full amount. Note that the cheese is not added until just before serving.

Makes 2 180-calorie servings, 2 generous cups each.

1/4 cup rinsed and drained canned kidney beans

1/4 cup chopped canned mild green chiles

1/4 cup bottled salsa or picante sauce

2 Tbsp chopped pitted black Kalamata olives, plus 2 Tbsp olive brine

1 1/2 tsp extra virgin olive oil

1 cup chopped fresh tomatoes

1/2 cup chopped sweet red or green bell pepper

4 cups coarsely chopped iceberg lettuce

1 Tbsp shredded or grated reduced-fat Cheddar cheese

1. In a large nonreactive bowl, thoroughly stir together beans, green chiles, salsa, olives, brine, and oil.

2. Add tomatoes, peppers, and lettuce, and toss until well combined.

Serve immediately or refrigerate, covered, for up to 2 days. Just before serving, sprinkle top with cheese.

Nutrition Facts

Serving Size 2 cups (341g)
Servings Per Container 2

Amount Per Serving

Calories 180   Calories from Fat 50

	% Daily Value*
Total Fat 6g	**9%**
Saturated Fat 1g	**5%**
Trans Fat 0g	
Cholesterol 0mg	**0%**
Sodium 510mg	**21%**
Total Carbohydrate 28g	**9%**
Dietary Fiber 10g	**40%**
Sugars 8g	
Protein 9g	

Turkish Vegetable Salad

We travel frequently and love to bring back ideas for recipes from our trips across the U.S. and overseas. On a recent visit to Turkey, Ruth and her husband enjoyed a version of this tasty salad in the seaside town of Bodrum, while they sat at a waterfront café looking out at the boats in the sun-drenched harbor.

The salad has some similarities to Greek salads we've enjoyed, with the unexpected addition of corn. If possible, use high-quality imported black olives in the recipe.

Makes 2 170-calorie servings, about 1 3/4 cups each.

1 Tbsp extra-virgin olive oil

1 Tbsp fat-free chicken broth or bouillon or vegetable broth

2 tsp cider vinegar

1/4 tsp celery salt

1 cup very thinly sliced romaine lettuce (sliced crosswise)

1 1/2 cups *each* small cubes of tomato and cucumber (peeled)

1/2 cup cooked and cooled corn kernels

1 cup chopped sweet yellow or red pepper

1/4 cup thinly sliced green onion tops

2 Tbsp chopped imported Kalamata or similar black olives

Salt and pepper to taste

1. In a large nonreactive bowl, stir together olive oil, broth, vinegar, and celery salt.

2. Stir in lettuce, and stir to mix well. Stir in remaining vegetables and salt and pepper, to taste. Serve at once, or refrigerate 1 or 2 hours to allow flavors to blend.

Salad will keep in refrigerator for 1 or 2 days but is best served the day it is made.

Nutrition Facts

Serving Size 1 3/4 cups (360g)
Servings Per Container

Amount Per Serving

Calories 170   Calories from Fat 80

	% Daily Value*
Total Fat 9g	**14%**
Saturated Fat 1g	**5%**
Trans Fat 0g	
Cholesterol 0mg	**0%**
Sodium 350mg	**15%**
Total Carbohydrate 20g	**7%**
Dietary Fiber 5g	**20%**
Sugars 8g	
Protein 4g	

Zippy Apple Chopped Salad

This crunchy salad gets its zip from prepared horseradish and some protein from reduced-fat feta cheese. Although feta is naturally low in calories, we have used the reduced-fat option. Do use tart apples to lower the calorie count.

Tip: We've found a little dressing goes farther when it's mixed with the greens before adding the other ingredients.

Makes 4 110-calorie servings, about 1 1/4 cups each.

1 Tbsp extra-virgin olive oil

1 Tbsp fat-free chicken broth or bouillon or vegetable broth

1/2 tsp apple cider vinegar

1/2 tsp prepared horseradish

Salt and pepper to taste

2 cups thinly sliced romaine lettuce, cut crosswise

1/2 cup chopped parsley

2 cups (peeled or unpeeled) chopped crisp, flavorful apple cubes

1/2 cup chopped celery

1/2 cup reduced-fat feta cheese

1. In a large nonreactive bowl, combine oil, broth, vinegar and salt and pepper, if desired. Stir to mix well.

2. Add lettuce and parsley, and stir to coat.

3. Stir in apple and celery, then stir in cheese. Serve in individual salad bowls.

Salad will keep, covered, in refrigerator 2 or 3 days.

Nutrition Facts

Serving Size 1 1/2 cups (131g)
Servings Per Container 4

Amount Per Serving

Calories 110   Calories from Fat 50

	% Daily Value*
Total Fat 6g	**9**%
Saturated Fat 2g	**10**%
Trans Fat 0g	
Cholesterol 5mg	**2**%
Sodium 270mg	**11**%
Total Carbohydrate 11g	**4**%
Dietary Fiber 3g	**12**%
Sugars 7g	
Protein 4g	

Potato Cauliflower Salad

If you're craving potato salad, try this tasty combination of potatoes and cauliflower, which tastes just as good (really!) but cuts the calories considerably. (This is just one of several recipes that deliver remarkably savory results with unexpected ingredients.)

Tip: For a quick garnish, reserve some of the green onions and parsley, and sprinkle them over top just before serving.

Makes 3 110-calorie servings, about 3/4 cup each.

1 cup red-skin potato cubes (either unpeeled or peeled)

2 cups small cauliflower florets

3 Tbsp light mayonnaise

2 Tbsp reduced-fat buttermilk

1/2 tsp *each* dried thyme and basil leaves

1/8 tsp celery salt

1/2 cup chopped celery

2 Tbsp *each* thinly sliced green onion tops and chopped parsley

Lettuce leaves for serving, optional

1. Place potatoes in a small saucepan, and cover with water. Bring to a boil over high heat, reduce heat to medium, cover, and cook about 10 to 12 minutes, until potatoes are very tender when pierced with a fork. Cool under running water, and drain well.

2. While potatoes are cooking, place cauliflower in a 2-cup measure or microwave-safe bowl. Cover with wax paper, and microwave on high power 3 to 4 minutes, until cauliflower is partially cooked when pierced with a fork. Cool under running water, and drain well.

3. Meanwhile, in a medium-sized bowl, stir together mayonnaise, buttermilk, thyme, basil, and celery salt. Stir in potatoes, cauliflower, celery, green onion, and parsley. Serve on lettuce leaves, if desired, or cover and refrigerate.

Salad will keep in refrigerator, covered, 1 or 2 days.

Nutrition Facts

Serving Size 3/4 cup (170g)
Servings Per Container 3

Amount Per Serving

Calories 110   Calories from Fat 50

% Daily Value*

Total Fat 5g	**8%**
Saturated Fat 1g	**5%**
Trans Fat 0g	
Cholesterol 5mg	**2%**
Sodium 190mg	**8%**
Total Carbohydrate 14g	**5%**
Dietary Fiber 3g	**12%**
Sugars 4g	
Protein 3g	

Cauliflower "Couscous" Salad

In this hearty salad, ground cauliflower masquerades as couscous. And if you don't tell diners what they're really eating, they probably won't know.

Tip: Chop the cauliflower using a food processor. To cool after microwaving, spread it on a dinner plate, and refrigerate while making the rest of the salad.

Makes 5 60-calorie servings, about 1 cup each

3 cups ground cauliflower (about 4 cups florets)

2 Tbsp lemon juice

1 Tbsp extra-virgin olive oil

1 1/4 tsp Italian dried herb seasoning

1 cup tomato cubes

1 cup peeled cucumber cubes

1/2 cup chopped parsley leaves

1/4 cup sliced green onion tops

Salt and black pepper to taste

1. In a 4-cup measure, cover cauliflower with wax paper and microwave on high power, stirring once, until partially cooked, 3 to 4 minutes. Remove from microwave, and set aside to cool.

2. While cauliflower is cooling, in large nonreactive bowl, stir together lemon juice, oil and seasoning.

3. Stir cooled cauliflower into dressing. Stir in tomato, cucumber, parsley onion, and salt and pepper to taste.

Serve immediately, or cover and refrigerate for later use. Salad will keep in refrigerator for 2 or 3 days.

Nutrition Facts

Serving Size 1 cup (170g)
Servings Per Container 5

Amount Per Serving

Calories 60   Calories from Fat 30

	% Daily Value*
Total Fat 3g	5%
Saturated Fat 0g	0%
Trans Fat 0g	
Cholesterol 0mg	0%
Sodium 30mg	1%
Total Carbohydrate 8g	3%
Dietary Fiber 2g	8%
Sugars 3g	
Protein 2g	

Spicy Eggplant-Lentil Salad

In parts of the Middle East and North Africa, it's sometimes said that women should know 99 ways to cook eggplant before they marry. Even if you already have the requisite 99 recipes, we hope you'll add this savory, Middle-Eastern-inspired vegetarian main-dish salad to your collection. The eggplant lends an appealing meatiness (but few calories); the lentils provide a bit of protein and chew; and the spices and condiments spark them both.

This dish does take more time than many in the book, but the eggplant-lentil mixture can be prepared well ahead and stashed in the refrigerator or freezer for a very convenient meal on diet days. Its flavor actually seems to improve with storage.

Makes 4 130-calorie servings, about 1 cup salad, plus vegetable garnishes, each serving.

1 large eggplant (about 20 oz), peeled, trimmed and cut into 1-inch cubes (enough to yield 4 cups)

1/4 cup bottled mild or medium-hot tomato salsa or taco sauce

1 Tbsp *each* extra-virgin olive oil and reduced-sodium soy sauce

2 tsp mild or medium-hot chili powder

1 tsp mild or medium-hot curry powder

1/2 cup cooked and cooled (unseasoned) red lentils or brown lentils*

1 1/3 cup finely diced celery

4 cups torn romaine leaves or other leafy lettuce leaves for serving

1 cup red or yellow tomato wedges for serving

Sweet green pepper slices or chopped green onions for garnish, optional

1. Spread eggplant cubes on a large microwave-safe plate. Sprinkle lightly with water. Cover with a microwave-safe cover or wax paper.

2. Microwave on high power for 2 minutes. Stir to redistribute cubes, then microwave about 2 to 3 minutes longer, stopping and stirring at 1-minute intervals, until cubes are barely tender when pierced with a fork. Drain eggplant well; pat dry with paper towels.

3. In a large, deep nonreactive bowl, thoroughly stir together salsa, oil, soy sauce, chili powder, curry powder, lentils, and eggplant until well blended. Let stand so flavors can blend for 5 to 10 minutes. If serving immediately or refrigerating, stir in celery. Or, if freezing for later use, omit celery, and stir it in after mixture has thawed.

4. At serving time, divide eggplant-lentil mixture into 4 portions. Serve them on romaine, garnished with tomato wedges. Add green pepper strips, if desired.

Serve immediately, or store covered and refrigerated for up to 4 days; or pack filling mixture airtight and store up to 1 month. Thaw and add celery just before serving.

*To cook lentils: In a medium saucepan, combine 1/2 cup picked over and rinsed red or brown lentils with 11/2 cups water. Bring to a boil over medium-high heat. Adjust heat so lentils boil gently; and cook, covered and stirring occasionally, for 10 to 15 minutes or until just tender and soft but not mushy. (Red lentils take considerably less time than brown ones.) They may be readied up to 2 days ahead and refrigerated, or frozen for up to 1 month (thaw before using). Freeze any leftover lentils for later use.

Nutrition Facts

Serving Size 1 cup (273g)
Servings Per Container 4

Amount Per Serving

Calories 130   Calories from Fat 40

% Daily Value*

Total Fat 4.5g   7%

Saturated Fat 0g   0%

Trans Fat 0g

Cholesterol 0mg   0%

Sodium 240mg   10%

Total Carbohydrate 18g   6%

Dietary Fiber 8g   32%

Sugars 6g

Protein 6g

Zesty Coleslaw

We've trimmed preparation time for this healthful, zippy slaw by relying on a package of ready-to-use unseasoned cabbage slaw mix. We've cut calories and fat by skipping the more typical, heavier mayo-laden dressing and opting for a simple vinegar and oil blend. And finally we've cranked up the taste by incorporating a little Dijon-style mustard, chopped green onions, and whole mustard and celery seeds. The slaw (pictured along with a sandwich in our Canadian Bacon, Lettuce, and Tomato Sandwich recipe, page 143) is also a nice accompaniment to many of the skillets, stews, and other sandwiches in the book.

Tip: For a slightly sweeter, tamer slaw, you could add in a packet of sugar substitute along with the sugar.

Makes 5 60-calorie servings, about 1 cup each.

3 Tbsp unseasoned rice vinegar

2 Tbsp chopped green onions (including tender green tops) or chopped fresh chives

1 Tbsp granulated sugar

1 Tbsp corn oil, canola oil, or safflower oil

1 1/2 tsp Dijon-style prepared mustard

1/4 tsp *each* mustard seed and celery seed

1/4 tsp salt

1 14-oz package ready-to-use cabbage coleslaw mix

Freshly ground black pepper to taste

1. In a large nonreactive bowl, thoroughly stir together vinegar, green onions, sugar, oil, prepared mustard, mustard seed, celery seed, and salt.

2. Add slaw to bowl, tossing until lightly coated with dressing; dressing will seem a bit skimpy at first, but just keep tossing and it will gradually cover slaw. Add ground black pepper to taste. For best flavor let slaw stand a few minutes before serving.

Serve immediately or cover and refrigerate for up to 4 days. Just before serving, stir well to recombine ingredients.

Nutrition Facts

Serving Size 1 cup (97g)
Servings Per Container 5

Amount Per Serving

Calories 60	Calories from Fat 25

	% Daily Value*
Total Fat 3g	**5%**
Saturated Fat 0g	**0%**
Trans Fat 0g	
Cholesterol 0mg	**0%**
Sodium 170mg	**7%**
Total Carbohydrate 7g	**2%**
Dietary Fiber 2g	**8%**
Sugars 3g	
Protein 1g	

Tomatoes Oregano

When plump, ripe, right-from-the-vine tomatoes are in season, they are almost sumptuous enough to make a whole diet-day lunch. Here we enhance them with oregano, which in our opinion complements them even better than today's most popular choice, basil. Dried oregano will do in this recipe, but if you have the fresh herb, the flavor will be quite extraordinary.

To round out the meal, we suggest adding a little wedge of reduced-fat cheese and a couple multigrain crackers (gluten-free if preferred). These extras aren't calorie freebies though, so be sure to check labels and add in the totals to the salad numbers for your meal.

Tip: We like the salad best when the tomatoes are served peeled, although this step is optional. The following method makes it super-easy: Spear each tomato with a fork at the stem end, then dunk in boiling water for 30 to 40 seconds or until the skins start to split and loosen. Let cool slightly. The skins will just pull right off. For convenience, you can peel the tomatoes ahead, then keep them refrigerated for up to 24 hours.

Makes 4 90-calorie servings, 4 or 5 (dressed) thick tomato slices each.

1/4 cup red wine vinegar or unseasoned rice vinegar

1 1/2 Tbsp extra-virgin olive oil

3/4 tsp granulated sugar or sugar substitute of your choice

1 Tbsp chopped fresh chives or chopped green onion, including tender tops

1 1/2 Tbsp finely chopped fresh oregano or 1 tsp dried oregano leaves

1/8 tsp celery seed, optional

1/4 tsp *each* salt and black pepper, or to taste

5 large sun-ripened red or yellow tomatoes, peeled or unpeeled and cored, or a mixture of the 2

Oregano, chive or garlic chive sprigs and blossoms, and fresh parsley leaves for garnish, optional

1. In a 1-cup glass measure, stir together vinegar, oil, sugar, chives, oregano, celery seed (if using), salt, and pepper until well blended. Use immediately or refrigerate for later use. Bring almost to room temperature before using.

2. Slice tomatoes crosswise into generous 1/3-inch-thick slices. Arrange a layer of them on a nonreactive serving plate, then drizzle some dressing over them. Top with another layer of tomatoes, then drizzle with more dressing. Repeat until all slices and dressing are used.

3. Serve immediately or cover and refrigerate up to 8 hours before serving. At serving time, garnish with oregano, chive or garlic chive sprigs or blossoms, and/or parsley leaves, if desired.

Dressed tomatoes will keep, covered and refrigerated, up to 8 hours.

Nutrition Facts

Serving Size 4 thick slices (250g)
Servings Per Container 4

Amount Per Serving

Calories 90   Calories from Fat 50

	% Daily Value*
Total Fat 6g	**9%**
Saturated Fat 1g	**5%**
Trans Fat 0g	
Cholesterol 0mg	**0%**
Sodium 160mg	**7%**
Total Carbohydrate 9g	**3%**
Dietary Fiber 3g	**12%**
Sugars 6g	
Protein 2g	

Marinated Cucumbers

This quick, easy and refreshing vegetable side dish is so low in calories that we enjoy it often. It's best with fresh dill, but you can also use dried dill weed.

If you wish to use sugar in this recipe, the cucumbers will have 27 calories per serving.

Tip: Most supermarkets stock fresh dill and other herbs in the produce section.

Makes 4 15-calorie servings, about 1/2 cup each.

3 Tbsp cold water

1 1/2 Tbsp apple cider vinegar

3 tsp sugar substitute (or 1 Tbsp sugar, if preferred)

1 Tbsp chopped fresh dill weed or 1/2 teaspoon dried dill weed

Dash salt and pepper

2 cups peeled and thinly sliced cucumber (about 1 medium)

1. Mix together water, vinegar, sugar substitute (or sugar), dill, salt and pepper in a shallow, 9 1/2" x 6 1/4" or similar nonreactive baking dish. Add cucumber slices, and stir to coat with dressing.

2. Cover with plastic wrap, and refrigerate 2 to 3 hours before serving, stirring occasionally.

Cucumber salad will keep in the refrigerator, covered, 2 or 3 days.

Nutrition Facts

Serving Size 1/2 cup (92g)
Servings Per Container 4

Amount Per Serving

Calories 15	Calories from Fat 0

	% Daily Value*
Total Fat 0g	0%
Saturated Fat 0g	0%
Trans Fat 0g	
Cholesterol 0mg	0%
Sodium 35mg	1%
Total Carbohydrate 3g	1%
Dietary Fiber 1g	4%
Sugars 2g	
Protein 1g	

CHAPTER 4 – MAIN DISHES WITH MEAT, POULTRY, & SEAFOOD

Guilt-Free Chili

Beef & Mushroom Pasta Sauce over Spaghetti Squash

Sausage and Sauerkraut Skillet

Sausage Hash

Kale, Vegetable, and Ham Stew

White Chili

Singapore Noodles with Chicken

Ginger Shrimp and Vegetables Skillet

Greek-Style Fish Skillet

Dilled Fresh Salmon-Potato-Vegetable Stew

Creamed Tuna

Cioppino

Guilt-Free Chili

Yes, this chili has a lot less beef than typical recipes—which means it has a lot fewer calories—but it seems beefy and satisfying, nonetheless. Our secret is to substitute chopped mushrooms for some of the usual beef, then to boost the meaty flavor by slipping in a little concentrated beef bouillon base or beef bouillon granules.

One brand of beef base that is fairly readily available in supermarkets is called "Better than Bouillon." We feel this paste-like product does indeed have a richer flavor than the usual bouillon granules, although the latter can be used if necessary. In either case, we recommend the reduced-sodium versions, as the "regular" ones are exceedingly salty.

Note that the recipe calls for canned, diced tomatoes that come already seasoned.

Makes 4 150-calorie servings, 1 1/8 cups each.

4 oz extra-lean ground beef

2 cups finely chopped mushrooms

3/4 cup *each* finely chopped onion and celery

2 to 4 tsp mild to medium chili powder, to taste

1 tsp *each* dried oregano leaves and ground allspice

3 to 5 Tbsp canned chopped green chiles, to taste

1 14.5-oz can diced tomatoes (seasoned with basil, garlic, and oregano), including juice

1 8-oz can tomato sauce

1 tsp reduced-sodium beef bouillon base or beef bouillon granules dissolved in 1 Tbsp hot water

1 cup drained, canned red kidney beans

Chopped onion and sweet red pepper for garnish, optional

1. In a medium-sized, heavy, nonreactive saucepan, over medium heat, stir together beef, mushrooms, onion, and celery. Cook, constantly stirring and breaking up beef, until it is lightly browned all over, 6 or 7 minutes.

2. Thoroughly blend chili powder, oregano, and allspice into mixture and cook, stirring, 1 minute longer. Stir in green chiles, tomatoes, tomato sauce, bouillon-water mixture, and kidney beans. Adjust heat so mixture simmers gently, and cook, covered, about 10 minutes longer so flavors can blend.

3. Serve immediately, or cover and refrigerate for later use. Garnish servings with chopped onions and sweet peppers, if desired.

Chili will keep, covered and refrigerated, for up to 4 days, or frozen for up to 3 weeks.

Nutrition Facts

Serving Size 1 1/8 cup (325g)
Servings Per Container 4

Amount Per Serving

Calories 150   Calories from Fat 15

	% Daily Value*
Total Fat 2g	**3%**
Saturated Fat 0.5g	**3%**
Trans Fat 0g	
Cholesterol 15mg	**5%**
Sodium 810mg	**34%**
Total Carbohydrate 22g	**7%**
Dietary Fiber 7g	**28%**
Sugars 7g	
Protein 12g	

Beef & Mushroom Pasta Sauce over Spaghetti Squash

Yes, we admit it! Spaghetti squash will never pass for actual spaghetti taste-wise, even though the two do look fairly similar. But this squash is a nice pasta stand-in because it has a very mild, fresh flavor that allows any full-bodied tomato pasta sauce to shine. And, truthfully, spaghetti squash not only fits our diet-day budget much better but is far more tempting than the several low-calorie pastas we've tried. Another plus of the squash: When prepared using the method here, it's actually easier to cook than most pastas!

Spaghetti squashes range in size from about 2 to 6 pounds. Buy a small one, if possible. If only large ones are available, prepare just as directed except increase the microwaving time, and keep frequently checking for doneness. Save whatever amount of squash is left over by packing it in storage bags and freezing for later use.

To keep preparations streamlined, the recipe calls for a 26-ounce jar of pasta sauce. Use any bottled tomato-based pasta sauce you like that has 50 or fewer calories per 1/2 cup (or substitute a calorie-wise homemade sauce). Otherwise, the calorie count will be higher than that listed in our recipe.

Tip: For a vegetarian sauce, omit the beef, increase the mushrooms to 3 cups, and substitute vegetable broth for the beef broth called for. In this case, the calorie count per serving will be 165.

Makes 4 190-calorie servings, 1 cup spaghetti squash and scant 1 cup sauce each.

3 oz extra-lean ground beef

1 2/3 cups sliced fresh mushrooms

1/2 cup peeled and chopped onion

2 tsp olive oil

1 tsp dried thyme leaves

2/3 cup fat-free, reduced-sodium beef broth

1 24-ounce jar commercial tomato-based pasta sauce

1 small spaghetti squash (2 pounds, if possible)

1 1/2 Tbsp shredded or grated Parmesan cheese for garnish

1. In a large nonreactive Dutch oven or soup pot, stir together beef, mushrooms, onion, olive oil, and thyme over medium heat. Cook, stirring and breaking up beef, about 6 minutes, or until mushrooms and beef are lightly browned.

2. Stir in broth, scraping up any bits of beef from pot bottom; and cook, stirring, 3 minutes to concentrate flavors. Stir in pasta sauce. Adjust heat so sauce simmers gently; cover and cook, stirring once or twice, for 5 to 10 minutes, then set aside.

3. Meanwhile, pierce whole squash deeply with a sharp knife in 5 or 6 places to create steam vents. Put squash on a microwave-safe plate. Top with a domed microwave cover or wax paper, and microwave on high power for 5 minutes. Start testing for doneness by poking squash with a paring knife; and, if necessary, continue microwaving until flesh feels just tender.

4. Let squash sit until cool enough to handle, then split in half lengthwise. Scrape out and discard seeds. Using a fork, scrape along squash interior, loosening and fluffing up lengths of squash. You'll need 4 loosely packed cups of squash; pack any extra in storage bags, and refrigerate or freeze for later use.

5. In a serving bowl toss squash with 1/2 cup of pasta sauce and 1/2 tablespoon Parmesan. Divide squash among 4 serving plates, then top each serving with a quarter of remaining sauce. Garnish serving tops with remaining 1 tablespoon Parmesan and serve.

Cooked spaghetti squash keeps well covered and refrigerated for up to 3 days. Sauce keeps well covered and refrigerated for up to 5 days. Both squash and sauce may also be frozen airtight for up to 1 month. Drain squash well before using.

Nutrition Facts

Serving Size 2 cups (427g)
Servings Per Container 4

Amount Per Serving

Calories 190   Calories from Fat 50

% Daily Value*

Total Fat 6g   **9%**

Saturated Fat 1g   **5%**

Trans Fat 0g

Cholesterol 15mg   **5%**

Sodium 550mg   **23%**

Total Carbohydrate 28g   **9%**

Dietary Fiber 6g   **24%**

Sugars 13g

Protein 10g

Sausage and Sauerkraut Skillet

Caraway, a key flavoring component in most seeded rye breads, also adds aroma and robust taste to this hearty skillet.

Tip: You can find fresh sauerkraut in plastic bags in the supermarket deli section. We call for turkey sausage because it's lower in fat than beef or pork sausage.

Makes 3 180-calorie servings, about 1 cup each.

6 oz reduced-fat turkey kielbasa (or similar) sausage

2 tsp olive oil

1 cup canned diced tomatoes

1 1/2 cups fresh sauerkraut, drained

1 tsp caraway seeds

1 to 2 tsp sugar substitute, to taste, optional

1/8 tsp black pepper

Chopped fresh chives or parsley for garnish, optional

1. Cut sausage into thin rounds. In a large nonstick nonreactive skillet over medium heat, cook sausage in oil until slightly browned, about 6 to 7 minutes, stirring frequently.

2. Add tomatoes, sauerkraut, caraway seeds, sugar substitute (if using), and pepper. Stir to mix well. Bring to a boil. Reduce heat, cover, and simmer about 15 minutes until flavors are well blended.

3. Garnish with chives or parsley, if desired, before serving.

Sausage and Sauerkraut Skillet will keep, covered and refrigerated, for 2 to 3 days.

Nutrition Facts

Serving Size 1 cup (267g)
Servings Per Container 3

Amount Per Serving

Calories 180   Calories from Fat 100

% Daily Value*

Total Fat 11g	**17%**
Saturated Fat 4g	**20%**
Trans Fat 0g	
Cholesterol 35mg	**12%**
Sodium 1430mg	**60%**
Total Carbohydrate 9g	**3%**
Dietary Fiber 3g	**12%**
Sugars 4g	
Protein 10g	

Sausage Hash

We love a homey meal of hash and vegetables and wanted to see if we could make a diet-day version. We did it by substituting ground cauliflower for a lot of the potato and using only a little reduced-fat or lean sausage. The hash goes nicely with our Caraway Cabbage. The sausage you need is the bulk kind, not the type that comes packed in casings.

Tip: We've shortened the cooking time considerably by starting the hash in the microwave.

Makes 2 170-calorie servings, about 1 cup each.

1 cup grated peeled or unpeeled red-skin potato (about 1 medium)

2 cups cauliflower florets, finely chopped

2 oz reduced-fat or light pork sausage

1/2 tsp dried herb poultry seasoning

1/4 tsp salt

Dash black pepper

1. In a medium-sized microwave-safe bowl, combine potato, cauliflower, and sausage. Use edge of a large spoon to crumble and stir sausage into potato mixture. Stir in seasonings.

2. Cover with wax paper, and microwave on high power 5 minutes, stopping and stirring once, until potatoes are partially cooked when tested with a fork.

3. Spray a nonstick skillet with nonstick spray. Over medium heat, brown hash mixture, stirring frequently, about 8 to 10 minutes, until potatoes begin to brown and are cooked.

Serve immediately, or cover and refrigerate for later use.

Nutrition Facts

Serving Size 1 cup (243g)
Servings Per Container 2

Amount Per Serving

Calories 170   Calories from Fat 50

	% Daily Value*
Total Fat 6g	**9%**
Saturated Fat 2g	**10%**
Trans Fat 0g	
Cholesterol 20mg	**7%**
Sodium 520mg	**22%**
Total Carbohydrate 23g	**8%**
Dietary Fiber 4g	**16%**
Sugars 3g	
Protein 9g	

Kale, Vegetable, and Ham Stew

Like most stews, this one can be made ahead and then quickly reheated for an easy diet-day meal. It includes a variety of the hardy, nutrient-rich winter vegetables, including fresh kale, turnips, cabbage, and cauliflower. These team up well with, and help stretch, the ham and potatoes—which keeps the overall calorie count quite reasonable.

Makes 4 150-calorie servings, a generous 1 1/8 cups each.

3 cups fat-free, low-sodium chicken broth

2 cups lightly packed fresh kale, torn from ribs and coarsely chopped

1 cup *each* cubed (1/3 inch) unpeeled Red Bliss potatoes, or other boiling potatoes, and turnips or rutabagas

2/3 cup *each* coarsely sliced carrots and celery

1/4 cup chopped green onions, including tender tops

1 tsp caraway seed

7 oz 97-percent lean, reduced-sodium smoked ham steak, trimmed of rind and cut into 1/3-inch cubes

1 cup *each* small cauliflower florets and coarsely chopped green cabbage

1. Stir together broth, kale, potatoes, turnips, carrots, celery, onions, caraway seeds and ham in a 4-quart (or similar) large pot. Bring to a boil, then adjust the heat so mixture boils gently.

2. Cover and cook, 9 to 12 minutes or until kale and potatoes are just barely tender when pierced with a fork. If needed to prevent liquid from boiling down, replenish by adding some hot water.

3. Stir in cauliflower and cabbage. Re-cover and simmer until cauliflower and cabbage are just tender, about 3 minutes longer. Serve immediately, or cover and refrigerate.

Stew keeps, covered, in refrigerator for up to 4 days.

Nutrition Facts

Serving Size 1 1/8 cup (401g)
Servings Per Container 4

Amount Per Serving

Calories 150   Calories from Fat 25

% Daily Value*

Total Fat 3g	**5%**
Saturated Fat 1g	**5%**
Trans Fat 0g	
Cholesterol 20mg	**7%**
Sodium 1050mg	**44%**
Total Carbohydrate 17g	**6%**
Dietary Fiber 4g	**16%**
Sugars 4g	
Protein 14g	

White Chili

White chili is a nice change of pace from the traditional version, and it's also a good choice if you're trying to eat less red meat. Like regular chili, it can be made well ahead, then stashed in the fridge or freezer and reheated for a convenient diet-day meal-in-a-bowl lunch or supper.

Tip: Even canned green chiles that are labeled "mild" can sometimes be quite piquant. So, unless you always like your food spicy, taste them before adding in the whole container.

Tip: Throughout the book, when recipes call for acidic or peppery ingredients, from tomatoes and chilies to vinegar and lemon juice, directions tell you to use "nonreactive" cooking and storage containers to ensure that the ingredients won't react with the pot and develop off flavors or odd color. Glass, ceramic, stainless steel, enamel-coated cast iron, anodized aluminum, and plastic are all nonreactive. Uncoated aluminum, cast iron, and copper will all react and begin to corrode in the presence of acids or peppery ingredients, so shouldn't be used.

4 190-calorie servings, scant 1 cup each.

2 tsp olive oil

1 6-oz boneless, skinless chicken breast half, cut into 1/2-inch cubes

1 cup chopped onion

3/4 cup *each* chopped celery and chopped cauliflower

1 small garlic clove, finely chopped

1 1/4 tsp *each* dried oregano leaves, dried basil leaves, and ground cumin

1 1/2 cups fat-free, reduced-sodium chicken broth

1 tsp cornstarch stirred together with 2 Tbsp water

1 4-oz can chopped mild green chiles, including juice

1 cup canned great Northern beans, including liquid

2 1/2 Tbsp fat-free sour cream, divided

1 Tbsp shredded reduced-fat Jack cheese or white Cheddar cheese for garnish, optional

1. In a large, nonreactive saucepan or medium pot, stir together oil, chicken, onion, celery, and cauliflower. Place over medium heat and cook, stirring, until well blended.

2. Stir in garlic, oregano, basil, and cumin. Cook, stirring, until chicken turns opaque and vegetables are soft, about 8 minutes.

3. Stir in broth, cornstarch-water mixture, green chiles, and beans. Bring to a boil, then adjust heat so chili boils gently. Cook, uncovered, stirring once or twice, for 10 to 12 minutes, or until liquid boils down slightly and flavors blend.

4. Remove from heat, and thoroughly stir in 1 1/2 tablespoons sour cream. Serve immediately, or cover and refrigerate for later use. If reheating, heat only to piping hot, *not boiling* as overheating can cause sour cream to curdle. Serve in soup plates or bowls. Garnish with little dollops of remaining 1 tablespoon sour cream, dividing it equally among servings. Also, garnish servings lightly with cheese, if desired.

White chili keeps, covered, in a nonreactive container refrigerated for 4 days, and frozen for up to 1 month.

Nutrition Facts

Serving Size 1 cup (303g)
Servings Per Container 4

Amount Per Serving

Calories 190   Calories from Fat 60

% Daily Value*

Total Fat 7g	**11%**
Saturated Fat 1.5g	**8%**
Trans Fat 0g	
Cholesterol 30mg	**10%**
Sodium 540mg	**23%**
Total Carbohydrate 18g	**6%**
Dietary Fiber 6g	**24%**
Sugars 3g	
Protein 15g	

Singapore Noodles with Chicken

This zesty, satisfying recipe calls for Asian rice noodles, also known as rice sticks. They are stocked in the ethnic section of many supermarkets and are particularly handy if you are going gluten-free. You could substitute 1/2 cup thin pasta noodles in a pinch, but note that they will need to be cooked al dente before being added. For a gluten-free recipe, be sure to use a gluten-free soy sauce.

Tip: The chicken is easier to cut into matchstick strips if partially frozen first.

Makes 3 190-calorie servings, about 1 1/4-cups each.

2 1/2 Tbsp light soy sauce

1 Tbsp mild or medium hot curry powder

1 cup fat-free chicken broth, divided

1 to 2 tsp peeled and finely minced ginger root, to taste

1 Tbsp toasted sesame oil

1 oz (about 1/2 cup) dry rice noodles (broken into 2 1/2-inch-long pieces before measuring)

1 boneless, skinless, medium chicken breast (6 oz), trimmed and cut into thin (1/16-inch-thick) and 2-inch-long strips

1 12-oz bag rainbow slaw (or 4 cups regular cabbage-carrot slaw)

2 to 3 scallions, trimmed of roots and tough green tops and cut into thin 2-inch-long shreds, divided

1. Combine soy sauce, curry powder, 1/2 cup chicken broth, ginger root, and sesame oil in a large bowl. Stir in chicken, and let stand 5 minutes. Meanwhile cover noodles with hot water, and let stand for 5 minutes.

2. Using a slotted spoon, transfer chicken to a 12-inch nonstick skillet.

3. Drain noodles well, and stir them into marinade used for chicken. Cook chicken, stirring, until just barely cooked through, about 2 to 3 minutes.

4. Add noodles, any remaining marinade, bag of slaw, and about 3/4 of scallion shreds to skillet.

5. Cook, stirring, until mixture is just cooked through, about 3 minutes longer; if mixture is dry, stir in enough more chicken broth to moisten and prevent burning.

Serve immediately. Just before serving, garnish with some remaining scallion shreds. Or cover and refrigerate for up to 3 days. If desired, cut more scallion shreds for garnish.

Nutrition Facts

Serving Size 1 1/4 cups (267g)
Servings Per Container 3

Amount Per Serving

Calories 190   Calories from Fat 60

% Daily Value*

Total Fat 7g	**11%**
Saturated Fat 1g	**5%**
Trans Fat 0g	
Cholesterol 35mg	**12%**
Sodium 700mg	**29%**
Total Carbohydrate 15g	**5%**
Dietary Fiber 3g	**12%**
Sugars 0g	
Protein 17g	

Ginger Shrimp and Vegetables Skillet

You'll need fresh ginger for this quick and easy Asian-inspired shrimp skillet. For a little extra zip, serve the dish sprinkled with a few thin strips of fresh ginger and some sliced green onions.

Tip: Be sure to use a gluten-free soy sauce, if you have a gluten sensitivity.

Makes 2 160-calorie servings, about 1 cup each.

2 Tbsp light soy sauce

2 tsp unseasoned rice vinegar or white wine vinegar

2 tsp peeled and minced fresh ginger

1 tsp peeled and chopped fresh garlic

1 tsp toasted sesame oil

2 to 3 drops Sriracha hot chili sauce or other hot pepper sauce

1/2 cup thinly sliced celery (cut on a diagonal)

1/2 cup canned, drained, diced water chestnuts

1 1/2 cups small broccoli or cauliflower florets (or a combination)

1/4 cup sliced green onion tops (cut on a diagonal), plus more for garnish

1 cup peeled, deveined, fresh medium-sized shrimp

1. In a medium-sized skillet, stir together soy sauce, vinegar, ginger, garlic, sesame oil, and Sriracha sauce. Cook over medium heat, stirring occasionally, 1 to 2 minutes, to allow flavors to blend.

2. Stir in celery, water chestnuts, broccoli, green onions, and shrimp. Raise heat, then adjust it so that sauce simmers.

3. Cook for 3 minutes, stirring, until vegetables are crisp tender and shrimp are just pink and cooked through.

Serve immediately, garnished with chopped onions and fresh ginger shreds, if desired.

Nutrition Facts

Serving Size 1 cup (288g)
Servings Per Container 2

Amount Per Serving

Calories 160   Calories from Fat 20

% Daily Value*

Total Fat 2.5g	**4%**
Saturated Fat 0g	**0%**
Trans Fat 0g	
Cholesterol 230mg	**77%**
Sodium 1900mg	**79%**
Total Carbohydrate 10g	**3%**
Dietary Fiber 3g	**12%**
Sugars 4g	
Protein 24g	

Greek-Style Fish Skillet

Fish is a great way to get your protein without adding a lot of calories to a meal. Here the strong flavors of classic Greek cuisine—artichokes, olives and feta cheese—add a full-bodied note to the dish.

Tip: Cutting up the fish into chunks speeds the cooking process and makes for a more attractive presentation.

Makes 2 170-calorie servings, about 1 1/2 cups each.

6 oz perch, pollock, or turbot fillets, cut into bite-sized pieces

1/2 cup canned artichoke heart quarters, drained, coarse outer leaves removed, and coarsely chopped

1 cup chopped canned tomatoes

1 oz (2 generous Tbsp) crumbled reduced-fat feta cheese

5 small pimiento-stuffed olives, sliced

1/2 tsp Italian dried herb seasoning

1. Spray a medium-sized nonstick skillet with nonstick spray. Add fish and cook over medium heat, turning once, until fish has turned opaque on both sides.

2. Add artichokes, tomatoes, feta, olives, and Italian seasoning, and stir to mix well. Bring to a boil, and reduce heat. Cook, uncovered, over medium heat, about 5 minutes, or until fish pieces are just cooked through and flavors are blended.

Fish skillet will keep in the refrigerator, covered, 1 or 2 days.

Nutrition Facts

Serving Size 1 1/2 cups (285g)
Servings Per Container 2

Amount Per Serving

Calories 170   Calories from Fat 30

	% Daily Value*
Total Fat 3g	5%
Saturated Fat 1g	5%
Trans Fat 0g	
Cholesterol 85mg	28%
Sodium 840mg	35%
Total Carbohydrate 12g	4%
Dietary Fiber 2g	8%
Sugars 5g	
Protein 22g	

Dilled Fresh Salmon-Potato-Vegetable Stew

Fresh dill weed has an unusual, refreshing herbal taste that brings out the best in both potatoes and salmon, and it adds a special dimension to this fragrant Scandinavian-inspired stew. Wait until you can find fresh, feathery dill to make the recipe, as dried dill weed is bland and just doesn't have enough oomph for good results.

Tip: Be sure to check along the fleshy side of the salmon fillet, and remove any bones along the lateral line before adding it to the pot.

Makes 4 190–calorie servings, about 1 1/8 cups each.

1 tsp corn oil or canola oil

1/2 cup *each* peeled and chopped carrot and diced celery

4 cups fat-free reduced-sodium chicken broth, divided

3 Tbsp fresh chopped chives or green onions, plus more for garnish, if desired

1 8-oz fresh or frozen (thawed) boneless north Atlantic salmon fillet (skin intact)

1 cup 1-inch cubes peeled or unpeeled boiling potatoes

1 1/2 cups *each* fresh or frozen (thawed) small cauliflower florets and very coarsely chopped green cabbage

1/3 cup chopped fresh dill weed (coarse stems removed), plus more for garnish, if desired

2 tsp prepared mustard, preferably Dijon-style

Salt and freshly ground black pepper to taste, optional

1. In a 4-quart nonreactive saucepan or similar-size soup pot, combine oil, carrot, and celery. Cook over medium-high heat, stirring frequently, 3 to 4 minutes, until vegetables just begin to brown. Add salmon, searing 1 to 2 minutes on flesh side, then laying it skin-side down.

2. Add 2 1/2 cups broth and chives, and adjust heat so mixture simmers. Poach salmon fillet, uncovered, for 6 to 10 minutes or until almost cooked through. Transfer it, skin-side up, to a cutting board and let cool. Meanwhile, add remaining 1 1/2 cups broth and potatoes to pot; boil gently, uncovered, for 10 minutes or until potatoes just begin to soften when pierced with a fork.

3. Stir cauliflower, cabbage, dill weed, and mustard into pot; if broth has boiled down or thickened, replenish it with up to a cup of water. Boil gently, uncovered, stirring once or twice, until potatoes are just tender, about 5 minutes longer.

4. Meanwhile, peel off and discard salmon skin. Cut flesh into generous 1-inch chunks, and return it to pot. Heat just until piping hot. Serve immediately, garnished with more fresh chopped dill weed, or cover and refrigerate for later use.

Keeps, covered and refrigerated, for up to 3 days.

Nutrition Facts

Serving Size 1 1/8 cups (408g)
Servings Per Container 4

Amount Per Serving

Calories 190   Calories from Fat 80

	% Daily Value*
Total Fat 9g	**14%**
Saturated Fat 2g	**10%**
Trans Fat 0g	
Cholesterol 30mg	**10%**
Sodium 590mg	**25%**
Total Carbohydrate 12g	**4%**
Dietary Fiber 3g	**12%**
Sugars 3g	
Protein 15g	

Creamed Tuna

Creamed Tuna over toast, another home-style dish, makes a satisfying lunch or dinner entrée. Be sure to use water-packed tuna.

Tip: Be sure to use "light" bread with 40 to 45 calories a slice.

Tip: If you are gluten-free, substitute your favorite gluten-free bread. Since "light" (40 to 45 calories per slice) gluten-free versions are very hard to find, you'll likely need to do a little math and either reduce the amount of bread in the recipe or add the extra calories (over 40 a slice) contributed by the brand you substitute.

Makes 2 170-calorie servings, about 1/2 cup plus 1 slice toast each.

1/2 cup reduced-fat milk (2% fat)

1 Tbsp cornstarch

2 Tbsp fat-free half and half

4 oz chunk white water-packed tuna, drained

2 Tbsp thinly sliced green onion tops

1/8 tsp celery salt, or to taste

2 slices "light" bread, toasted

1. Thoroughly stir together milk and cornstarch in medium-sized pot, until well blended. Add half and half, stirring to mix well.

2. Stir tuna, onion, and celery salt into pot. Place over medium-high heat, and cook, stirring, just until mixture thickens and flavors are blended, about 3 minutes.

3. Place toast on serving plates. Spoon tuna mixture over top, and serve.

The tuna mixture will keep in the refrigerator, covered, 1 or 2 days.

Nutrition Facts

Serving Size 1/2 cup plus bread (149g)
Servings Per Container 2

Amount Per Serving

Calories 170   Calories from Fat 40

	% Daily Value*
Total Fat 4.5g	7%
Saturated Fat 1.5g	8%
Trans Fat 0g	
Cholesterol 35mg	12%
Sodium 490mg	20%
Total Carbohydrate 16g	5%
Dietary Fiber 1g	4%
Sugars 4g	
Protein 17g	

Cioppino

Festive and slightly fancy, this full-flavored seafood stew is a fine choice when you want to serve calorie-conscious company or to treat yourself on a diet day. It's best to use fresh rather than frozen shrimp, though good-quality frozen fish will do. If you can find already-debearded mussels, preparations will go a bit faster.

Makes 4 200-calorie servings, a generous 1 cup sauce plus about 1/2 cup of fish and shellfish each.

1 tsp olive oil

1/2 cup *each* chopped onions and celery

1 14.5-oz can diced, seasoned tomatoes (seasoned with basil, garlic, and oregano), including juice

2 cups fat-free reduced-sodium chicken broth

1 8-oz can tomato sauce

1 tsp *each* dried thyme leaves and chili powder

1 large bay leaf

Pinch hot red pepper flakes, optional

12 *each* fresh mussels and fresh, unpeeled medium shrimp

8 oz fresh (or frozen, thawed) skinless, boneless cod, haddock, or other firm, mild white fish fillet, cut into 4 pieces

Lemon wedges and chopped parsley for garnish, optional

1. In a 4-quart or larger heavy pot or 4-quart nonreactive saucepan, stir together olive oil, onions, and celery. Cook over medium heat, stirring, until onion is lightly browned, about 5 minutes.

2. Stir in tomatoes, chicken broth, tomato sauce, thyme, chili powder, bay leaf, and red pepper flakes (if using). Bring mixture to a boil, then adjust the heat so it simmers gently. Cook, stirring, uncovered, until mixture cooks down and flavors blend, 10 to 15 minutes.

3. Meanwhile, thoroughly scrub and then wash mussels in several changes of water. Using kitchen shears or sharp knife, trim away and discard any dark bits of beard. Also discard any mussels with broken shells or that are not tightly closed. Rinse well and drain. Peel and devein shrimp, leaving tails intact, if desired.

4. Stir mussels into pot liquid. Cook, stirring once or twice, for 2 minutes. Immediately stir in shrimp, then add in and push fish portions down into the liquid until partially covered. Cover, and cook until shrimp turn pink and fish portions look opaque in thickest part when flaked with a fork, about 4 minutes longer. Discard any mussels that have not opened. Discard bay leaf.

5. Arrange mussels, shrimp, and fish in 4 soup plates, dividing equally among them. Ladle tomato-vegetable mixture over top, dividing equally among servings. Serve with lemon wedges and chopped with parsley, if desired.

Keeps covered and refrigerated in a nonreactive container for up to 36 hours. Reheat over low heat, stirring occasionally just until piping hot; serve immediately.

Nutrition Facts

Serving Size 1 1/2 cups (467g)
Servings Per Container 4

Amount Per Serving

Calories 200   Calories from Fat 30

% Daily Value*

Total Fat 3g	**5%**
Saturated Fat 0.5g	**3%**
Trans Fat 0g	
Cholesterol 110mg	**37%**
Sodium 970mg	**40%**
Total Carbohydrate 11g	**4%**
Dietary Fiber 2g	**8%**
Sugars 6g	
Protein 31g	

CHAPTER 5 – SANDWICHES

Tuna Sandwich

Egg Salad Sandwich

Canadian Bacon, Lettuce, and Tomato Sandwich

Ham and Cheese Sandwich

Middle Eastern Hummus-Veggie Sandwich Wrap

Onion and Sweet Pepper Quesadilla

Tuna Sandwich

"Light" or reduced-carb bread is a boon, if you don't want to give up eating sandwiches on diet days. In case you aren't familiar with it, light bread comes in various white, multigrain, and whole-wheat versions, and most brands have only 40 to 45 calories a slice. It looks and tastes more or less like regular sandwich bread, but does have a decidedly airier, less substantial texture. Of course, that airiness and the slightly thinner slices are what account for the fewer calories!

We also call for light mayonnaise in this recipe and have used one with 35 calories a tablespoon. If you choose a reduced-fat mayo with a different number, just adjust the total calories per serving up or down as necessary.

Tip: For a much lighter diet-day meal, simply serve the tuna salad over leafy greens and skip the bread entirely. In which case, subtract 80 calories for the bread, and add 15 for the extra lettuce.

Tip: If you are gluten-free, substitute your favorite gluten-free bread or make open-faced sandwiches using rice cakes or corn cakes (thins). However, be sure to check the calorie counts of these products. Since the product will likely not have the 40-45 calories of "light" bread, you'll need to do a little math and add or subtract calories to get your final count.

Makes 2 200-calorie sandwiches, half of filling and two slices of 40-calorie light bread each.

2 Tbsp light mayonnaise

1/2 cup finely chopped celery

1 1/2 Tbsp *each* finely chopped dill pickle and chopped green onion

1 tsp Dijon-style mustard

1 5-oz can water-packed, solid white Albacore tuna, drained

4 slices (40 calories each) multigrain "light" sandwich bread

4 large, torn romaine leaves or other crisp lettuce leaves

1. In a medium nonreactive bowl stir together mayonnaise, celery, pickle, green onion, and mustard until well blended. Stir in tuna until thoroughly incorporated. Use tuna salad right away, or refrigerate, airtight, until serving time.

2. At serving time, divide tuna in half, and spread each portion on a slice of bread. Cover tuna generously with lettuce leaves, then top each with a second slice of bread. Cut sandwiches in half and serve.

Tuna salad will keep, covered and refrigerated, for up to 3 days.

Nutrition Facts

Serving Size 1 sandwich (179g)
Servings Per Container 2 sandwiches

Amount Per Serving

Calories 200	Calories from Fat 40

	% Daily Value*
Total Fat 4.5g	7%
Saturated Fat 0g	0%
Trans Fat 0g	
Cholesterol 30mg	10%
Sodium 420mg	18%
Total Carbohydrate 22g	7%
Dietary Fiber 3g	12%
Sugars 4g	
Protein 20g	

Egg Salad Sandwich

Instead of just eating plain hard-boiled eggs on diet days, turn them into a filling for an open-faced egg salad sandwich. (We like to use a slice of reduced-calorie toast or even a rice cake for the sandwich base.) Another option: Serve the egg salad on lettuce leaves with tomatoes and cucumber, or tuck it in half a sweet red pepper (which will save 25 to 45 calories per serving).

Tip: We keep dill pickle relish on hand to zip up this and other recipes; it's much lower in calories than regular pickle relish. But if you don't have dill pickle relish on hand, you can substitute chopped dill pickle.

Tip: If you are gluten-free, substitute rice cakes or corn cakes (thins). However, be sure to check the calorie counts of these products. Since they may not have the 40-45 calories of "light" bread, you'll need to do a little math and add or subtract calories to get your final count.

Makes 2 140-calorie servings, about 1/3 cup salad plus 1 slice bread each.

2 hard-cooked eggs, cooled, peeled, and chopped

1 Tbsp light mayonnaise

1 tsp dill pickle relish

1/4 tsp Dijon-style mustard, or to taste

2 Tbsp finely chopped celery

1. Combine egg, mayonnaise, relish, and mustard in a small bowl. Stir to mix well. Stir in celery.

2. Spread on toast slices and serve, or cover and refrigerate egg salad for later use.

Salad will keep, covered and refrigerated, for up to 2 days.

Nutrition Facts

Serving Size 1/3 cup salad plus 1 bread slice (86g)

Servings Per Container 2

Amount Per Serving

Calories 140　　Calories from Fat 70

% Daily Value*

Total Fat 8g	**12%**
Saturated Fat 2g	**10%**
Trans Fat 0g	
Cholesterol 215mg	**72%**
Sodium 360mg	**15%**
Total Carbohydrate 10g	**3%**
Dietary Fiber 1g	**4%**
Sugars 2g	
Protein 9g	

Canadian Bacon, Lettuce, and Tomato Sandwich

To bring down the calories in this classic sandwich, we used Canadian bacon. And we serve it on light multigrain English muffin halves, which have only 50 calories. Alternatively, you could use a slice of toasted light-style bread. And if you want to add a second slice of bread, you can do it for only 40 to 45 calories.

Tip: If you are gluten-free, substitute a rice cake or corn cake (thin) for an English muffin. Alternatively, use a gluten-free English muffin, and adjust the calorie count. Since "light" (40 to 50 calories per half muffin) gluten-free versions are very hard to find, you'll likely need to do a little addition or subtraction to determine the final calorie count.

Makes 2 150-calorie servings, 1 open-faced sandwich each

4 oz (about 6 slices) Canadian bacon

1 light multigrain English muffin

6 thin red or yellow tomato slices, or a combination of the 2

2 romaine lettuce leaves–folded in half

1. Cook bacon according to package directions and set aside.

2. Carefully split the muffin in half. Lightly toast the halves.

3. Set each muffin half on a plate. Arrange bacon on top. Add tomato and lettuce. Serve with Zesty Coleslaw, as shown, if desired.

Sandwich can be wrapped airtight and refrigerated for up to 2 days.

Nutrition Facts

Serving Size 1 open-faced sandwich (199g)

Servings Per Container 2

Amount Per Serving

Calories 150   Calories from Fat 40

	% Daily Value*
Total Fat 4.5g	**7%**
Saturated Fat 1.5g	**8%**
Trans Fat 0g	
Cholesterol 30mg	**10%**
Sodium 590mg	**25%**
Total Carbohydrate 18g	**6%**
Dietary Fiber 5g	**20%**
Sugars 3g	
Protein 15g	

Ham and Cheese Sandwich

Yes, you can have a ham and cheese sandwich on a diet day, if you do it right. One secret is using light multigrain English muffins, which have only 50 calories per half. You could use reduced-calorie bread for your open-faced sandwiches, if you prefer, of course.

Tip: If you are gluten-free, substitute a rice cake or corn cake (thin) for an English muffin. Alternatively, use a gluten-free English muffin, and adjust the calorie count. Since "light" (40 to 50 calories per half muffin) gluten-free versions are very hard to find, you'll likely need to do a little addition or subtraction to determine the final calorie count.

Makes 2 140-calorie servings, 1 open-faced sandwich each.

1 light multigrain English muffin or 2 slices light multigrain bread, toasted

1/4 cup shredded reduced-fat sharp Cheddar cheese (made with 2% milk)

4 oz very thinly sliced deli ham

4 thin red or yellow tomato slices (or a combination)

Mustard and dill pickle slices for garnish, if desired

1. Carefully split muffin in half horizontally. Lightly toast halves. Sprinkle cheese on top, and melt in a toaster oven or in microwave oven on medium power for 20 to 30 seconds.

2. Arrange each muffin half on a plate. Top with ham and tomato slices. Serve with mustard and thin dill pickle strips, if desired.

Sandwich can be wrapped airtight and refrigerated for up to 2 days.

Nutrition Facts

Serving Size 1 open faced sandwich (213g)

Servings Per Container 2

Amount Per Serving

Calories 140   Calories from Fat 40

	% Daily Value*
Total Fat 4g	6%
Saturated Fat 2g	10%
Trans Fat 0g	
Cholesterol 30mg	10%
Sodium 880mg	37%
Total Carbohydrate 18g	6%
Dietary Fiber 4g	16%
Sugars 3g	
Protein 16g	

Middle Eastern Hummus-Veggie Sandwich Wrap

Sometimes really quick, easy recipes sacrifice taste for convenience; but, trust us, this simple sandwich wrap delivers a lot of eating pleasure for a very modest effort. When Nancy finished making our final version, she planned to eat only half the wrap and put the other portion away for later. Instead, however, she polished off the whole thing! The good news— whether you choose to make two mini-meals or one substantial meal of the wrap, it fits nicely into the diet-day food budget.

Tip: Flour tortillas come in several sizes and styles with wildly different calorie counts. For this recipe you need a "low-carb" medium-sized (8-inch-diameter) soft-flour tortilla that has about 80 calories per round. Also, you can choose either a regular or spicy hummus made from beans, eggplant, artichoke, or sweet peppers; but be sure the product has 25 or fewer calories per tablespoon to ensure that your actual calorie count matches the numbers here.

Tip: If you follow a gluten-free diet, substitute gluten-free tortillas, and adjust the final calorie count of the recipe.

Makes 1 180-calorie sandwich wrap, 2 4-inch-wrap halves per serving.

10 to 12 peeled, thin cucumber slices

1 8-inch-diameter "low-carb" soft-flour tortilla

2 1/2 Tbsp regular or spicy hummus

2 Tbsp *each* finely chopped fresh parsley and sweet red or green pepper

4 or 5 medium-sized thin tomato slices

1. Lay cucumber slices on paper towels. Top with more paper towels, patting down lightly. Let stand so moisture can be absorbed while you complete remaining tasks.

2. On a large plate, lay out tortilla, and spread hummus thinly but evenly over it. Sprinkle chopped parsley and sweet pepper over hummus. Arrange cucumber slices evenly over surface, patting them down firmly. Lightly pat tomato slices dry with paper towels, then arrange them evenly over cucumbers.

3. Roll up wrap from one side like a burrito, tucking in open ends of tortilla to hold ingredients in. Cut wrap in half on a diagonal and serve, or refrigerate, well wrapped, for later use.

Wrap can be made ahead and kept refrigerated, wrapped airtight, for up to 6 hours. It will lose crispness and gradually grow soggy over longer storage.

Nutrition Facts

Serving Size 1 8-inch wrap (271g)
Servings Per Container 1

Amount Per Serving

Calories 180   Calories from Fat 50

% Daily Value*

Total Fat 6g	**9%**
Saturated Fat 0g	**0%**
Trans Fat 0g	
Cholesterol 0mg	**0%**
Sodium 560mg	**23%**
Total Carbohydrate 28g	**9%**
Dietary Fiber 12g	**48%**
Sugars 7g	
Protein 7g	

Onion and Sweet Pepper Quesadilla

For crunch and flavor, we've added peppers and onion to this classic Mexican cheese and tortilla sandwich. And we've speeded up the cooking process and eliminated fat by starting the onions and peppers in the microwave.

Tip: Be sure to read the label, and buy flour tortillas with 90 calories or fewer each.

Tip: If you follow a gluten-free diet, substitute gluten-free tortillas, and adjust the final calorie count of the recipe.

Makes 1 160-calorie serving, 1 tortilla with filling.

1 Tbsp chopped onion

2 Tbsp chopped yellow or green pepper

1 6-inch low-fat flour tortilla

3 Tbsp grated, reduced-fat Cheddar cheese (from 2-percent-fat milk)

2 Tbsp mild or medium bottled salsa

1. Combine onion and pepper in a 1-cup measure or microwave-safe bowl. Cover with wax paper, and microwave on high power 45 seconds to 1 minute until onions are partially cooked when tested with a fork.

2. Lay tortilla in a medium-sized skillet. Sprinkle evenly with cheese, spreading it out with back of a spoon. Then distribute onions and peppers evenly over cheese.

3. Heat to medium, cover skillet with lid, and cook until cheese is melted, about 2 to 3 minutes. Spoon salsa evenly over cheese and vegetables. Fold in half and serve. Or wrap airtight and refrigerate for later use; then cover and microwave to reheat wrap to warm.

Quesadilla will keep in refrigerator up to 2 days.

Nutrition Facts

Serving Size 1 quesadilla (103g)
Servings Per Container 1

Amount Per Serving

Calories 160   Calories from Fat 40

% Daily Value*

Total Fat 4.5g	**7%**
Saturated Fat 2.5g	**13%**
Trans Fat 0g	
Cholesterol 10mg	**3%**
Sodium 520mg	**22%**
Total Carbohydrate 22g	**7%**
Dietary Fiber 3g	**12%**
Sugars 3g	
Protein 9g	

CHAPTER 6 – VEGETABLE AND VEGETARIAN MAIN AND SIDE DISHES

Mock Pizza Omelet

Faux "Fried Rice"

Bean and Cheese Tostadas

Mushroom Stroganoff

Microwaved Vegetables with Parmesan Cheese

Portobello Slices

Asparagus Stir-Fry with Toasted Sesame Seeds

Cabbage with Caraway

Moroccan-Style Winter Squash and Garbanzo Bean Stew

Green Beans Amandine

Roasted Wax Beans with Feta, Lemon Zest, and Herbs

Mock Pizza Omelet

This recipe delivers the taste of pizza but eliminates the calories normally contributed by a crust. We just cover a flat omelet with pizza toppings, and voilà. The microwave oven speeds preparation, and liquid egg substitute keeps the calorie count down.

Tip: If you don't have pizza sauce, you can substitute marinara sauce combined with a quarter teaspoon of oregano.

Makes 2 150-calorie servings, 1/2 omelet each.

1 cup liquid egg substitute

1/2 cup pizza sauce

1/4 cup shredded reduced-fat mozzarella cheese

1 Tbsp shredded or grated Parmesan cheese

1. Spray a medium-sized nonstick skillet with nonstick spray. Add the egg substitute, and cook over medium heat. As egg cooks, lift edges with a plastic spatula, and tip pan slightly to let uncooked portions flow underneath.

2. When top of egg is set, about 6 minutes, reduce heat to medium low. Spoon sauce over top, and spread it out with back of a large spoon. Sprinkle on cheeses. Cover with pan lid, and cook just until the mozzarella melts, about 2 to 3 minutes. Remove from heat.

3. With edge of a plastic spatula, cut omelet into quarters, making four "pizza" slices. Using a wide plastic spatula, carefully lift slices onto plates and serve.

Mock pizza slices may be covered and refrigerated for up to 2 days. Rewarm on 50-percent power for 20 to 30 seconds; be careful not to overheat.

Nutrition Facts

Serving Size 1/2 omelet (201g)
Servings Per Container 2

Amount Per Serving

Calories 150   Calories from Fat 30

	% Daily Value*
Total Fat 3.5g	5%
Saturated Fat 2g	10%
Trans Fat 0g	
Cholesterol 10mg	3%
Sodium 730mg	30%
Total Carbohydrate 9g	3%
Dietary Fiber 1g	4%
Sugars 4g	
Protein 18g	

Faux "Fried Rice"

This is good example of how cauliflower can easily substitute for a higher-calorie ingredient. There's no rice in this Asian-influenced dish. The grains are all ground cauliflower, and it's surprisingly difficult to detect that you are not eating the real thing. For an extra 90 calories, you can stir in 2 ounces of chopped, thinly sliced chicken breast meat for a Faux "Chicken Fried Rice."

Tip: To cut preparation time, finely chop the cauliflower in a food processor.

Makes 2 110-calorie servings, 2 cups each.

1/2 cup liquid egg substitute

Salt and pepper to taste

3 cups finely chopped cauliflower (about 4 cups florets)

1/4 cup thinly sliced green onion tops

1/2 cup thinly sliced celery, sliced on the diagonal

2 1/2 Tbsp light soy sauce (or more to taste)

2 tsp rice vinegar or white wine vinegar

1 tsp toasted sesame oil

2 to 3 drops hot pepper sauce

1. Place cauliflower in a four-cup measure, cover with wax paper, and microwave on high power, stopping and stirring once, until partially cooked, 3 to 4 minutes.

2. Meanwhile, in a medium-sized nonstick skillet sprayed with nonstick spray, combine egg substitute and salt and pepper. Cook over medium heat, stirring occasionally, until consistency of scrambled eggs is reached. Remove from skillet; set aside in a small bowl.

3. In same skillet, combine soy sauce, vinegar, and sesame oil. Stir in cauliflower, onion, celery, and hot pepper sauce. Cook over medium heat, stirring frequently, 3 or 4 minutes, until flavors are blended. Stir in cooked egg substitute. Serve immediately, or cover and refrigerate for later use. Reheat in microwave oven on 50-percent power, about 30 seconds, or just until hot before serving.

Faux "Fried Rice" will keep in refrigerator up to 2 days.

Nutrition Facts

Serving Size 2 cups (255g)
Servings Per Container 2

Amount Per Serving

Calories 110   Calories from Fat 25

	% Daily Value*
Total Fat 2.5g	4%
Saturated Fat 0g	0%
Trans Fat 0g	
Cholesterol 0mg	0%
Sodium 870mg	36%
Total Carbohydrate 13g	4%
Dietary Fiber 5g	20%
Sugars 8g	
Protein 11g	

Bean and Cheese Tostadas

There's just something about doing a lot of munching that helps keep you satisfied on diet days. So we like to keep around and nibble on flat, crisp corn-tortilla or tostada shells. These taste pretty much like corn chips but have proportionally fewer calories and less fat.

We eat the broken shells as is for a very light snack, but use the whole ones to make these easy, remarkably savory, vegetarian (and gluten-free) tostadas. (If you are imagining those humongous, piled high, greasy versions from fast food restaurants, you'll have to scale down your thinking; but, honestly, our lighter, healthier option is much more flavorful. It makes a very substantial snack or a light meal.)

Makes 1 120-calorie tostada, 1 serving.

1 6-inch plain, flat corn tortilla or tostada shell

2 Tbsp fat-free canned refried beans

2 Tbsp canned chopped green chiles or bottled roasted chopped red sweet peppers

1 Tbsp 2-percent-fat pepper Jack, Jack, or Cheddar cheese

2 Tbsp diced tomatoes

1 Tbsp freshly chopped green onions for garnish, optional

1. Lay tostada shell on a microwave-safe plate, and set aside briefly. In a small bowl, stir together beans and chiles until well blended. Evenly but gently spread bean mixture onto tostada shell, then sprinkle cheese over top.

2. Top tostada with microwave-safe cover. Microwave on 50-percent power for 50 to 60 seconds, or just until cheese mostly melts.

3. Immediately garnish top with tomatoes. Sprinkle on green onions, if desired.

Serve immediately, as the shell will lose its crispness upon standing.

Nutrition Facts

Serving Size 1 tostado (119g)
Servings Per Container 1

Amount Per Serving

Calories 120   Calories from Fat 15

% Daily Value*

Total Fat 1.5g	**2%**
Saturated Fat 0g	**0%**
Trans Fat 0g	
Cholesterol 0mg	**0%**
Sodium 280mg	**12%**
Total Carbohydrate 21g	**7%**
Dietary Fiber 3g	**12%**
Sugars 1g	
Protein 6g	

Mushroom Stroganoff

With only about 15 calories a cup, mushrooms make a great low-cal stroganoff. And while we're making this dish, we often snitch a couple of raw mushrooms to munch on. (We toss them into salads, too.)

Tip: This recipe calls for only a tablespoon of marinara sauce. If you don't happen to have an opened jar in the refrigerator, any leftover tomato-based pasta sauce or leftover tomato sauce can be substituted. In a pinch, you could even use catsup, though the calories will be a little higher.

Tip: Serve the stroganoff over a slice of "light" toast (40-45 calories) or, for a more substantial meal, serve it over some leftover pasta; note that 1/3 cup of cooked pasta will add about 75 calories to the dish. Still another possibility, if you are gluten-free: Serve it over 1/2 cup cooked spaghetti squash, which will add 40 calories.

Makes 2 70-calorie servings, about 1 cup each.

2 cups sliced white mushrooms

1/2 cup fat-free beef broth or bouillon or vegetable broth

1 Tbsp cornstarch

1/2 cup reduced-fat milk (2% fat)

1 Tbsp marinara sauce or tomato sauce

1/2 tsp Dijon-style mustard

1/8 tsp dried thyme leaves

Salt and white pepper to taste

1. In 8-inch or similar small skillet, combine mushrooms and broth. Cook over medium heat, stirring frequently, until mushrooms are cooked through and broth has partially cooked down, about 5 minutes.

2. Meanwhile, thoroughly stir cornstarch and milk together in a 2- cup measure. Stir marinara sauce, mustard, thyme leaves, and salt and pepper into milk mixture.

3. Add milk mixture to mushroom mixture, and bring back to a gentle boil, stirring constantly. Cook, stirring, until mixture just thickens, about 2 minutes.

4. Serve plain, or spoon serving over toast or pasta or spaghetti squash (or other low-calorie vegetable desired). Or refrigerate for later use.

Stroganoff will keep in refrigerator, covered, for 2 days.

Nutrition Facts

Serving Size 1 cup (204g)
Servings Per Container 2

Amount Per Serving

Calories 70   Calories from Fat 15

                                                    % Daily Value*

Total Fat 1.5g	**2%**
Saturated Fat 1g	**5%**
Trans Fat 0g	
Cholesterol 5mg	**2%**
Sodium 300mg	**13%**
Total Carbohydrate 9g	**3%**
Dietary Fiber 1g	**4%**
Sugars 5g	
Protein 5g	

Microwaved Vegetables with Parmesan Cheese

Although it's not a fancy dish, this quick and easy vegetable medley is one of our standard diet-day meals. It makes a great light lunch or dinner entrée or colorful, healthful vegetable side dish. Be sure to check labels, and use marinara sauce with 45 calories or fewer per serving.

Tip: You can vary the dish by substituting other low-calorie vegetables such as halved Brussels sprouts, mushrooms, or celery slices for some of the zucchini or cauliflower. We've found this is a good dish for using up vegetables that happen to be on hand in the refrigerator.

Makes 2 160-calorie servings, about 2 cups each.

3 cups mixed cauliflower and broccoli florets

3 cups large zucchini cubes

1/2 cup chopped green or red pepper

1/2 cup marinara sauce

Salt and pepper to taste

3 Tbsp shredded or grated Parmesan cheese

1. Combine vegetables in a large microwave-safe casserole or bowl. Cover with casserole top or wax paper, and microwave on high power, 3 to 4 minutes, stirring halfway through, until vegetables are partially cooked when tested with a fork.

2. Stir in marinara sauce, cover, and microwave another 1 to 3 minutes until vegetables are tender.

3. Stir in most of Parmesan and salt and pepper, if desired. Garnish with remaining Parmesan, and serve.

Dish will keep in refrigerator, covered, for 2 or 3 days.

Nutrition Facts

Serving Size 2 cups (365g)
Servings Per Container 2

Amount Per Serving

Calories 160   Calories from Fat 50

% Daily Value*

Total Fat 6g	**9%**
Saturated Fat 2.5g	**13%**
Trans Fat 0g	
Cholesterol 15mg	**5%**
Sodium 540mg	**23%**
Total Carbohydrate 19g	**6%**
Dietary Fiber 8g	**32%**
Sugars 7g	
Protein 9g	

Portobello Slices

Mushrooms are so low in calories that they fit perfectly into diet days. If you like portobellos, you'll love these pan-grilled slices, tossed with a little balsamic vinegar and Parmesan cheese.

Makes 2 45-calorie servings, 4 slices each.

4 oz portobello mushroom slices (about 8 slices from 1 large mushroom)

1 tsp olive oil

Salt to taste

1/8 tsp black pepper

1 tsp balsamic vinegar

1 tsp shredded or grated Parmesan cheese

1. Spray coat a medium-sized nonstick skillet with nonstick spray. Add mushrooms to skillet, and brush with oil, using a brush or paper towel. Sprinkle with salt and pepper, if desired.

2. Cook over medium to medium-high heat 7 to 8 minutes, turning once or twice, or until mushrooms have softened and have begun to brown.

3. Remove pan from heat. Stir in vinegar and cheese, and toss to coat mushrooms. Serve at once.

Mushrooms may be stored, covered and refrigerated for up to 2 days.

Nutrition Facts

Serving Size 4 slices (62g)
Servings Per Container 2

Amount Per Serving

Calories 45   Calories from Fat 20

	% Daily Value*
Total Fat 2.5g	**4%**
Saturated Fat 0g	**0%**
Trans Fat 0g	
Cholesterol 0mg	**0%**
Sodium 15mg	**1%**
Total Carbohydrate 3g	**1%**
Dietary Fiber 1g	**4%**
Sugars 1g	
Protein 2g	

Asparagus Stir-Fry with Toasted Sesame Seeds

We cook asparagus often when it's in season, sometimes by braising or roasting it, sometimes in this Asian-inspired dish. The quick cooking preserves the flavor, color, and slightly crunchy texture of the vegetable, and the toasted sesame seeds and sesame oil lend a bit more texture and rich taste without too many calories. It's a good diet-day side dish, but on occasion, we've made a whole meal of it by eating two servings instead of one!

Tip: Don't confuse oriental toasted sesame oil with the light-colored and mild-tasting sesame oil that is available in health food stores. Dark or toasted sesame oil has a distinct nutty flavor and rich brown color. It's usually stocked near the soy sauce in grocery stores.

Tip: If you are gluten-sensitive, be sure to use gluten-free soy sauce.

Makes 4 70–calorie servings, about 3/4 cup each.

1 1/2 pounds fresh asparagus (untrimmed)

1 Tbsp hulled sesame seeds

2 tsp *each* corn oil and toasted sesame oil

2 tsp reduced-sodium soy sauce or regular soy sauce

Coarsely-ground gourmet-blend peppercorns for garnish, optional

1. Break off and discard tough ends from asparagus spears; reserving top 5 to 6 inches for use. Cut spears on a diagonal into 1 1/2-inch pieces.

2. In a 12-inch or similar nonstick skillet over medium-high heat, toast sesame seeds, stirring constantly, 2 or 3 minutes, or until they just begin to turn light brown. Watch carefully and immediately turn them out onto paper toweling.

3. In same skillet, heat corn oil to hot but not smoking. Add asparagus pieces, and adjust heat so they cook fairly briskly but don't burn. Cook, stirring constantly, 2 minutes or until pieces are almost crisp-tender when tested with a fork; add a teaspoon of water, if needed to prevent burning. Add sesame oil and soy sauce; cook, stirring, about 1 minute longer.

4. Transfer asparagus to serving dish. Garnish with sprinkling of coarsely-ground multi-blend peppercorns, if desired. Garnish with sesame seeds and serve.

Asparagus can be refrigerated, airtight, for up to 3 days.

Nutrition Facts

Serving Size 3/4 cup (100g)
Servings Per Container 4

Amount Per Serving

Calories 70 — Calories from Fat 50

	% Daily Value*
Total Fat 6g	9%
Saturated Fat 1g	5%
Trans Fat 0g	
Cholesterol 0mg	0%
Sodium 100mg	4%
Total Carbohydrate 4g	1%
Dietary Fiber 2g	8%
Sugars 2g	
Protein 3g	

Cabbage with Caraway

Because it's so low in calories, cabbage is a handy way to add texture and volume to many of our diet-day dishes. But here it's a memorable side dish, enlivened by the rich flavor of caraway. Because the cabbage is cooked in the microwave, it's ready in minutes. We like to serve it with our Sausage Hash.

Makes 2 50-calorie servings, about 3/4 cup each

4 cups thinly-sliced green cabbage

1/2 cup tomato sauce

2 Tbsp fat-free chicken broth or bouillon or vegetable broth

1/2 tsp caraway seeds

Salt and pepper to taste

1. Stir together cabbage, tomato sauce, broth, and caraway seeds in a 4-cup measure or microwave-safe bowl.

2. Cover with wax paper, and microwave on high power, 5 or 6 minutes, stopping and stirring once, until cabbage is tender when tested with a fork. Add salt and pepper to taste, and serve.

Dish will keep in refrigerator, covered, 2 or 3 days.

Nutrition Facts

Serving Size 3/4 cup (216g)
Servings Per Container 2

Amount Per Serving

Calories 50   Calories from Fat 5

% Daily Value*

Total Fat 0g   **0%**

   Saturated Fat 0g   **0%**

   Trans Fat 0g

Cholesterol 0mg   **0%**

Sodium 360mg   **15%**

Total Carbohydrate 11g   **4%**

   Dietary Fiber 4g   **16%**

   Sugars 1g

Protein 3g

Moroccan-Style Winter Squash and Garbanzo Bean Stew

Butternut squash is one of the most widely stocked large winter squashes in supermarkets and is a good choice for this fragrant stew. It and some other large winter squash varieties are sometimes sold already peeled and cubed; and, since their rind and flesh are hard to cut, the ready-to-use packages can be great time-savers.

But not to worry! If you can only find whole squash, you can still greatly speed preparations simply by microwaving a few minutes to soften the hard flesh before you peel and cube it. Choose a butternut, Hubbard, or similar squash (or half) weighing about 1 2/3 pounds. Pierce it deeply with a sharp knife in 5 or 6 places to create steam vents. Put the squash on a microwave-safe plate, drape wax paper over top, and microwave on high power for about 4 minutes. Start testing it by poking with a paring knife, and, if necessary, continue microwaving until the skin and flesh are barely tender enough to facilitate cutting. Let the squash sit until cool enough to handle, then cut the flesh into 1-inch cubes.

Tip: If you are a fan of Moroccan food and happen to keep preserved lemons around, serve them, chopped, in a condiment bowl along with the finished stew. They will add a lot of zestiness but only a couple calories per serving. This makes a very satisfying diet-day vegetarian main dish.

Makes 4 180-calorie servings, 1 1/8 cups each.

4 cups coarsely cubed winter squash

2 tsp olive oil

1 cup peeled and chopped onion

1 1/2 tsp *each* ground coriander and finely minced fresh ginger root

1/4 tsp *each* ground turmeric and ground cumin

Pinch hot red pepper flakes or more to taste

1 14.5-oz can diced tomatoes including juice (plain or seasoned with green chiles)

1/3 cup seedless golden or brown raisins

1/4 tsp salt, or more to taste

1 cup canned garbanzo beans, rinsed well and drained

Fresh lemon wedges and fresh chopped coriander leaves for serving, plus chopped preserved lemons, optional

1. If using squash cubes that have not already been microwaved, place them slightly separated on a microwave-safe plate. Top with a microwave cover or wax paper. Microwave on high power, stopping and testing with a paring knife at 3 minutes and then 1 minute intervals until the flesh is just beginning to give. Set aside.

2. In a deep 12- or 13-inch skillet, heat olive oil and onion over medium heat, stirring. Cook onion, stirring, about 4 minutes or until lightly browned. Add microwaved squash, coriander, ginger, turmeric, cumin, and red pepper, stirring until squash cubes are completely coated with spices. Cook, stirring, 1 minute. Stir in tomatoes, raisins, and garbanzo beans.

3. Adjust heat so mixture boils gently, and cook, uncovered, until squash pieces are just tender and liquid has boiled down a bit, about 5 minutes. Taste and add salt if desired. If stew seems dry, stir in a little water. If desired, provide lemon wedges and chopped coriander leaves so diners can garnish their stew to taste. Set out chopped preserved lemons for garnishing, if desired.

Stew keeps well covered and refrigerated for up to 3 days. It may also be frozen airtight for up to 1 month.

Nutrition Facts

Serving Size 11/8 cup (316g)
Servings Per Container 4

Amount Per Serving

Calories 180   Calories from Fat 25

% Daily Value*

Total Fat 3g	**5%**
Saturated Fat 0g	**0%**
Trans Fat 0g	
Cholesterol 0mg	**0%**
Sodium 520mg	**22%**
Total Carbohydrate 36g	**12%**
Dietary Fiber 7g	**28%**
Sugars 14g	
Protein 5g	

Green Beans Amandine

We love Green Beans Amandine and were excited to find we could make this dish pretty much the way we always do as a diet-day side dish. Toasting the almonds in the microwave means you don't have to use any extra fat.

Makes 3 80-calorie servings, scant 1 cup each.

3 cups fresh green beans, stem ends removed and snapped in half

2 Tbsp sliced almonds

1/2 Tbsp butter

Salt to taste

1. In a medium saucepan, cover green beans with water. Bring to a boil, reduce heat, and boil gently for 8 to 12 minutes, depending on desired degree of doneness. When beans are tender, drain in a colander and return to pan.

2. Meanwhile, spread almonds on a small microwave-safe paper plate. Microwave on 100-percent power about 2 to 2 1/2 minutes, stopping and stirring every 30 seconds until browned but not burned. Set aside.

3. Stir butter into beans, and stir to coat evenly. Stir in nuts. Sprinkle with salt, if desired.

Beans can be stored, covered and refrigerated, for up to 2 days.

Nutrition Facts

Serving Size 1 cup (114g)
Servings Per Container 3

Amount Per Serving

Calories 80	Calories from Fat 35

	% Daily Value*
Total Fat 4g	**6%**
Saturated Fat 1.5g	**8%**
Trans Fat 0g	
Cholesterol 5mg	**2%**
Sodium 270mg	**11%**
Total Carbohydrate 9g	**3%**
Dietary Fiber 4g	**16%**
Sugars 2g	
Protein 3g	

Roasted Wax Beans with Feta, Lemon Zest, and Herbs

*This recipe was inspired by one in **The Glorious Vegetables of Italy**, (Chronicle Books, 2013) a handsome, well-crafted cookbook by Nancy's friend, Domenica Marchetti. It incorporates a technique often used in Italian cooking— livening a savory dish with a garlicky herb-lemon mixture called gremolata. We find this condiment particularly handy for diet days because it adds loads of flavor but few calories to a recipe.*

Here the fresh herb-zest blend is combined with lemon juice to create a vibrant-tasting dressing. Domenica presented the recipe in her sides chapter and suggested serving it warm, but we often eat it at room temperature or chilled as a light diet-day, main-dish salad. It's delightful!

The original recipe called for fresh wax beans, and they are excellent in the recipe. If you can't obtain them, it's fine to substitute regular green beans, although note that the lemon juice will tend to drab their color. If you are really pressed for time, you can substitute a bag of frozen whole wax or green beans for fresh. In this case, thaw them under warm water; pat **completely dry** *with paper towels; and reduce the roasting time to 5 to 10 minutes.*

Makes 3 120-calorie servings, about 1 1/3 cups each.

4 cups whole yellow wax beans or green beans, stem ends trimmed off

1 1/2 Tbsp extra-virgin olive oil

1/4 tsp salt, plus more to taste, optional

Gremolata Dressing and Cheese

2 Tbsp chopped fresh parsley

1 Tbsp *each* chopped chives and fresh mint or oregano

1 small garlic clove, peeled and finely minced or grated

Finely grated zest (yellow part of peel) and 2 Tbsp juice from 1 large lemon

2 Tbsp crumbled reduced-fat feta cheese

Halved cherry tomatoes and chopped purple basil leaves for garnish, optional

1. Preheat oven to 425 degrees F.

2. Put beans on a medium-sized rimmed baking sheet; add oil and salt, then stir until well coated. Spread out to form a single layer. Roast, uncovered, stirring once or twice, for 10 to 15 minutes or until beans are just tender when pierced with a fork.

3. Meanwhile in a large nonreactive bowl, stir together parsley, chives, mint (or oregano), garlic, lemon zest, and juice.

4. Add roasted beans to bowl with herbs, tossing until well blended. Taste and add more salt if desired. Let stand 5 to10 minutes to allow flavors to blend.

5. Serve immediately, or cover, refrigerate and serve lightly chilled. Garnish with feta just before serving. Garnish the tops with a few cherry-tomato halves and fresh purple basil, if desired.

Keeps well, covered and refrigerated, for up to 3 days.

Nutrition Facts

Serving Size 1 1/3 cups (141g)
Servings Per Container 3

Amount Per Serving

Calories 120   Calories from Fat 70

	% Daily Value*
Total Fat 8g	**12%**
Saturated Fat 1.5g	**8%**
Trans Fat 0g	
Cholesterol 0mg	**0%**
Sodium 270mg	**11%**
Total Carbohydrate 8g	**3%**
Dietary Fiber 3g	**12%**
Sugars 3g	
Protein 3g	

CHAPTER 7 – DIPS, DRESSINGS, AND CONDIMENTS

Russian Dressing

Spinach Dip

Creamy Ranch Dressing

Light Citrus Vinaigrette Dressing

Ginger-Honey Vinaigrette Dressing and Marinade

Blueberry Sauce

Russian Dressing

If you're in need of a snack, raw vegetables are great nibbles on diet days. This easy dressing will liven up everything from celery and carrot sticks, to sweet pepper and cucumber slices, while adding very few extra calories. It's also great on a tossed salad of greens. Or add lean cooked chicken breast meat or shrimp over the greens to create a meal. Russian Dressing is on the right in the above picture; the Spinach Dip (on the left above) recipe follows this one.

Makes 7 25-calorie servings, about 1 tablespoon each.

3 Tbsp catsup

2 Tbsp fat-free sour cream

2 Tbsp light mayonnaise

1 tsp prepared horseradish

1/8 tsp celery salt

1. In a small bowl, stir together catsup, sour cream, mayonnaise, horseradish and celery salt, and mix well.

2. Serve with selection of low-cal vegetables such as celery, radishes, cucumber, sweet peppers, green beans, or cauliflower.

Dressing will keep in refrigerator, covered, for 4 or 5 days.

Nutrition Facts

Serving Size 1 tablespoon (17g)
Servings Per Container 7

Amount Per Serving

Calories 25   Calories from Fat 15

% Daily Value*

Total Fat 1.5g	2%
Saturated Fat 0g	0%
Trans Fat 0g	
Cholesterol 0mg	0%
Sodium 135mg	6%
Total Carbohydrate 3g	1%
Dietary Fiber 0g	0%
Sugars 2g	
Protein 0g	

Spinach Dip

Here's another quick and tasty dip that will add flavor to raw vegetables such as carrots, celery, peppers, cucumber, radishes, and raw mushrooms. Spinach adds texture and volume to the dip but few calories. The Spinach Dip is shown next to the Russian Dressing in the picture above.

Tip: The recipe calls for onion powder which we like to keep on our spice shelf because it adds flavor without adding extra calories.

Tip: You can quickly thaw the spinach in the microwave on the defrost setting.

Makes 8 30-calorie servings, about 1 tablespoon each.

1/3 cup fat-free sour cream

3 Tbsp light mayonnaise

1/8 tsp celery salt

1/8 tsp onion powder

2 Tbsp thawed and drained chopped frozen spinach (about 1/4 cup frozen)

1. In a small bowl, stir together sour cream and mayonnaise. Stir in celery salt and onion powder. Stir in spinach and mix well. Serve with raw vegetables.

Dip will keep in the refrigerator, covered, for 3 or 4 days.

Nutrition Facts

Serving Size 1 tablespoon (19g)
Servings Per Container 8

Amount Per Serving

Calories 30	Calories from Fat 20

	% Daily Value*
Total Fat 2g	**3%**
Saturated Fat 0g	**0%**
Trans Fat 0g	
Cholesterol 5mg	**2%**
Sodium 70mg	**3%**
Total Carbohydrate 2g	**1%**
Dietary Fiber 0g	**0%**
Sugars 1g	
Protein 1g	

Creamy Ranch Dressing

Ranch dressing is definitely one of our favorites, so we were delighted to discover it's easy to make a low-calorie version with buttermilk. Use this dressing on greens or on a chunky vegetable salad.

Tip: Make sure the mayonnaise and buttermilk are thoroughly whisked together before adding the additional ingredients.

Makes 8 40-calorie servings, about 2 tablespoons each.

3/4 cup 2-percent-fat buttermilk, shaken well before using

1/4 cup light mayonnaise

1/2 tsp *each* dried thyme and basil leaves

1/2 tsp minced garlic

1/4 tsp celery salt

2 to 3 drops hot pepper sauce

1. In a medium-sized bowl, combine buttermilk and mayonnaise, and thoroughly whisk together. Check to make sure there are no lumps.

2. Stir in thyme, basil, garlic, celery salt, and hot pepper sauce. Serve at once, or cover and refrigerate.

Dressing will keep in refrigerator, covered, for up to a week.

Nutrition Facts

Serving Size 2 tablespoons (31g)
Servings Per Container 8

Amount Per Serving

Calories 40   Calories from Fat 25

	% Daily Value*
Total Fat 3g	**5%**
Saturated Fat 1g	**5%**
Trans Fat 0g	
Cholesterol 5mg	**2%**
Sodium 90mg	**4%**
Total Carbohydrate 2g	**1%**
Dietary Fiber 0g	**0%**
Sugars 1g	
Protein 1g	

Light Citrus Vinaigrette Dressing

Serve this light, citrusy vinaigrette over mixed greens or cooked broccoli or cauliflower.

Tip: If you prefer, substitute olive oil for the corn oil called for. Just remember that it will solidify in the refrigerator, so the vinaigrette will need to be brought to room temperature before serving. Also, the garlic is entirely optional; it will lend a mild, yet noticeable, garlicky flavor and aroma to the vinaigrette.

Makes 10 40-calorie servings, 1 tablespoon each.

1/3 cup orange juice

1 Tbsp clover honey

1 tsp Dijon-style grainy mustard

1/4 tsp *each* celery salt and finely grated fresh lemon zest (yellow part of peel)

1 thin slice fresh garlic, optional

1/4 cup unseasoned rice vinegar

2 1/2 Tbsp corn oil or safflower oil

1. In a small, deep, nonreactive bowl, whisk together orange juice, honey, mustard, celery salt, lemon zest, and garlic (if using) until thoroughly blended and free of any mustard clumps.

2. Whisk in vinegar, then gradually whisk in oil. For a mild garlic flavor remove and discard garlic slice; for more intense taste, leave it in dressing for a few hours, then discard.

Use dressing immediately or refrigerate, airtight, in a nonreactive container. Whisk or shake well just before serving.

Keeps, refrigerated, for up to 1 week.

Nutrition Facts

Serving Size 1 tablespoon (21g)
Servings Per Container 10

Amount Per Serving

Calories 40   Calories from Fat 30

% Daily Value*

Total Fat 3.5g	**5%**
Saturated Fat 0.5g	**3%**
Trans Fat 0g	
Cholesterol 0mg	**0%**
Sodium 70mg	**3%**
Total Carbohydrate 3g	**1%**
Dietary Fiber 0g	**0%**
Sugars 2g	
Protein 0g	

Ginger-Honey Vinaigrette Dressing and Marinade

This dressing is nice to have on hand to perk up a bowl of plain steamed or microwaved low-calorie vegetables, particularly bok choy, broccoli, or celery or a combo of these. (Uncooked, chopped bok choy has about 10 calories per cup, and chopped celery and broccoli each have about 15 calories per cup, so undressed these can almost be considered diet-day freebies!) Just drizzle a teaspoon or two of the dressing over the vegetables, and toss well right before serving.

The dressing is also called for in our Asian-Style Chicken-Apple Salad on page 69.

Tip: Toasted sesame oil is usually stocked in the Asian section of supermarkets. It has a rich brown color and distinctive nutty taste. Don't confuse it with regular sesame oil which is very mild and won't contribute the necessary flavor.

Makes 11 60-calorie servings, 1 tablespoon each.

1/3 cup unseasoned rice vinegar

3 1/2 Tbsp reduced-sodium soy sauce, gluten-free, if desired

1 1/2 Tbsp clover honey mixed with 1 1/2 Tbsp hot tap water

2 tsp prepared mustard

1 Tbsp peanut oil, corn oil, or safflower oil

2 tsp toasted sesame oil

1 tsp finely grated or minced peeled fresh gingerroot

Salt and freshly ground black pepper to taste, optional

1. In a 2-cup glass measure or small deep nonreactive bowl, stir together vinegar, soy sauce, honey-water mixture, mustard, peanut oil, sesame oil, and gingerroot.

2. Taste and stir in salt and pepper, if desired. Stir well right before using.

Serve immediately, or cover and refrigerate for up to 2 weeks.

Nutrition Facts

Serving Size 1 tablespoon (32g)
Servings Per Container 11

Amount Per Serving

Calories 60   Calories from Fat 20

% Daily Value*

Total Fat 2.5g   **4%**

Saturated Fat 0g   **0%**

Trans Fat 0g

Cholesterol 0mg   **0%**

Sodium 210mg   **9%**

Total Carbohydrate 10g   **3%**

Dietary Fiber 0g   **0%**

Sugars 9g

Protein 0g

Blueberry Sauce

We find this sauce to be a really fine accompaniment to our French Toast. It's also a quick, tasty way to dress up a cup of plain low-fat or fat-free yogurt or a serving of light cottage cheese. Note that if you prefer to omit the modest amount of sugar called for and use sugar substitute, depending on the brand, your sauce will have about 3 or 4 fewer calories per tablespoon.

Makes 10 15-calorie servings, a generous 1 tablespoon each.

1 1/4 tsp cornstarch

Generous 1/3 cup cold water

1/4 tsp freshly grated lemon zest (yellow part of peel)

1 cup fresh (or frozen, thawed) blueberries

1/2 tsp *each* fresh lemon juice and vanilla extract

1 Tbsp granulated sugar

1. Put cornstarch in a 1-quart saucepan. Gradually stir water into cornstarch until completely blended and smooth. Stir in lemon zest and blueberries.

2. Place over medium heat, and bring to a boil, stirring. Adjust heat so mixture boils gently, and cook, stirring, until blueberries are just soft and mixture is slightly thickened. Immediately remove from heat.

3. Stir in lemon juice and vanilla. Stir in sugar until thoroughly incorporated and dissolved. Set aside to cool to warm before serving.

Serve immediately, or cover and refrigerate in a nonreactive container. Keeps for up to 1 week.

Nutrition Facts

Serving Size 1 tablespoon (25g)
Servings Per Container 10

Amount Per Serving

Calories 15   Calories from Fat 0

% Daily Value*

Total Fat 0g	0%
Saturated Fat 0g	0%
Trans Fat 0g	
Cholesterol 0mg	0%
Sodium 0mg	0%
Total Carbohydrate 4g	1%
Dietary Fiber 0g	0%
Sugars 3g	
Protein 0g	

CHAPTER 8 – BREAKFASTS, SNACKS, AND DRINKS

French Toast

Ham and Spinach Scramble

Two-Minute "Baked" Egg 'n' Muffin Breakfast

Yogurt-Blueberry-Granola Breakfast Parfait

Mixed Berry Smoothie

Banana-Chocolate Breakfast Smoothie

Strawberry Lassi

Microwave "Grilled" Cheese Sandwich Snack

Microwave "Baked" Apples

Frozen Banana Chocolate-Peanut Pops

Pomegranate Pops

French Toast

This breakfast indulgence doesn't have to cost you a lot of calories, if you use reduced-calorie bread and liquid egg substitute. For a pretty presentation, you can serve it with either some strawberries or raspberries and a light syrup or with our Blueberry Sauce.

Tip: Since "light" bread is thin and fairly fragile, handle it carefully after soaking in the egg mixture.

Tip: Make sure the dish used to soak the bread slices can hold 4 slices lying flat. Also, you may want to use 2 spatulas to lift and turn the bread slices.

Tip: If you'd like to serve French toast for a snack, you may want to make half a recipe—or stash the extra slices airtight in the refrigerator to enjoy at another meal.

Tip: If you are gluten-free, substitute your favorite gluten-free bread. Since "light" (40 to 45 calories per slice) gluten-free versions are very hard to find, you'll likely need to do a little math and either reduce the amount of bread in the recipe or add the extra calories (over 40 a slice) contributed by the brand you substitute.

Makes 2 120-calorie servings, 2 slices each (not including fruit or sauce).

1/2 cup liquid egg substitute

3 Tbsp reduced-fat milk (2 percent fat)

1/2 tsp vanilla extract

Dash salt

4 slices light oatmeal or whole wheat bread (40-45 calories a slice)

Blueberry Sauce or berries and light syrup

1. In an 8" x 11" or similar oblong, flat-bottom baking dish, mix together egg substitute, milk, vanilla, and salt. Lay bread slices in mixture until egg mixture is partially absorbed. When about half egg mixture has been absorbed, carefully turn slices with 1 or 2 spatulas to coat on second sides.

2. Spray a large nonstick skillet with nonstick spray. Over medium heat, cook bread slices, turning once or twice with a plastic spatula, until lightly browned and cooked through, about 10-12 minutes. Serve with Blueberry Sauce or sugar-free syrup and berries, if desired.

Slices will keep, wrapped airtight and refrigerated, for up to 2 days. Reheat to warm in a microwave oven on 50-percent power for about 30 seconds before serving.

Nutrition Facts

Serving Size 2 slices (113g)
Servings Per Container 2

Amount Per Serving

Calories 120   Calories from Fat 5

	% Daily Value*
Total Fat 0.5g	1%
Saturated Fat 0g	0%
Trans Fat 0g	
Cholesterol 0mg	0%
Sodium 300mg	13%
Total Carbohydrate 20g	7%
Dietary Fiber 2g	8%
Sugars 4g	
Protein 11g	

Ham and Spinach Scramble

Because we've used liquid egg substitute in this tasty dish, it's easy to fix and low in calories. We serve it at either lunch or breakfast. Just a little ham and Parmesan cheese add a lot of flavor to the dish.

Makes 2 110-calorie servings, about 3/4 cup each.

1/2 cup frozen chopped spinach

3/4 cup liquid egg substitute

Salt and pepper, optional

1 oz leftover or deli ham, cut into small pieces

1 1/2 Tbsp shredded or grated Parmesan cheese

1. Thaw and drain spinach according to package directions (volume will reduce by half). Set aside.

2. Spray a medium-sized nonstick skillet with nonstick spray. Pour egg substitute into cold skillet, and sprinkle with salt and pepper, if desired. Heat skillet to medium. As egg substitute begins to cook, sprinkle spinach over top.

3. Gently stir mixture until scrambled. When it is almost cooked, stir in ham, and cook for about a minute longer to heat through. Sprinkle with Parmesan cheese, and serve.

Dish can be stored, covered, in refrigerator 1 or 2 days.

Nutrition Facts

Serving Size 3/4 cup (175g)
Servings Per Container 2

Amount Per Serving

Calories 110   Calories from Fat 25

% Daily Value*

Total Fat 3g	**5%**
Saturated Fat 1.5g	**8%**
Trans Fat 0g	
Cholesterol 15mg	**5%**
Sodium 560mg	**23%**
Total Carbohydrate 4g	**1%**
Dietary Fiber 1g	**4%**
Sugars 2g	
Protein 15g	

Two-Minute "Baked" Egg 'n' Muffin Breakfast

We have adapted this recipe from one shared with us by a friend, Eileen Buckholtz. On a busy diet-day morning it makes a nourishing, but nearly effortless, hot breakfast. As written, the recipe is vegetarian, but, for a slightly heartier meal, we occasionally toss a slice of diced, cooked Canadian bacon or 1 tablespoon leftover, lean ham into the egg mixture before baking. If you decide to do this, note that it will add about 40 more calories to the dish!

Tip: We sometimes cook an extra slice of Canadian bacon on regular days, then stash it in the refrigerator to add to our Egg 'n' Muffin meal.

Tip: If you are gluten-free, substitute a slice of your favorite gluten-free bread for the English muffin half, and adjust the calories of the recipe accordingly. ("Light" English muffins that are also gluten-free are very hard to find.)

Makes 1 120-calorie baked-egg breakfast dish, 1 baked egg and 1/2 light English muffin each.

1/3 cup liquid egg substitute

2 1/2 Tbsp shredded 2-percent-fat shredded sharp Cheddar cheese

1/8 tsp salt

Freshly ground black pepper to taste, optional

1 well-toasted "light" multigrain English muffin half

1. In a 1-cup measure stir together egg substitute, all but 1 teaspoon cheese, and salt. Spray a 1-cup (or slightly larger) glass custard cup with nonstick spray.

2. Pour egg mixture into custard cup. Place in microwave oven, and cover with microwave cover or wax paper. Microwave on 50-percent power for 1 minute. Then, checking for doneness at 20-second intervals, continue microwaving until egg puffs up and appears set except in very center (which should look barely runny).

3. Put toasted muffin on a serving plate. Run a table knife around and under baked egg to loosen it from cup. When egg is fully loosed, turn it out onto muffin half.

4. Garnish top with remaining 1 teaspoon shredded cheese and serve.

Serve immediately, as muffin will lose crispness and egg will become too firm upon standing.

Nutrition Facts

Serving Size 1 egg bake, 1 English muffin half (127g)

Servings Per Container 1

Amount Per Serving

Calories 120   Calories from Fat 15

% Daily Value*

Total Fat 1.5g	**2%**
Saturated Fat 1g	**5%**
Trans Fat 0g	
Cholesterol 5mg	**2%**
Sodium 640mg	**27%**
Total Carbohydrate 15g	**5%**
Dietary Fiber 4g	**16%**
Sugars 3g	
Protein 15g	

Yogurt-Blueberry-Granola Breakfast Parfait

We call this a "breakfast" parfait, but it would also make an eye-catching brunch dish. We borrowed the idea from a breakfast-tray parfait enjoyed at a fancy California spa.

The dish is easier to put together than you might guess and as gratifying as it looks. The keys to making it fit in a diet-day budget are to choose a fat-free "light and fit" sweetened vanilla yogurt (no more than 80 calories per 5.3-ounce cup) and to use only modest amounts of "light" granola and blueberry sauce. Interestingly, even the small quantities of these two lend lots of appealing fruit flavor and texture to the parfait.

Tip: While we call for our Blueberry Sauce (see page 200) in the recipe, you can substitute fresh blueberries—they're good, too. For a gluten-free parfait, just choose a gluten-free granola.

Makes 1 170-calorie serving, about 1 cup.

2 Tbsp Blueberry Sauce

5.3 oz. carton "light and fit" or similar nonfat, reduced-calorie vanilla-flavored yogurt

2 Tbsp reduced-fat granola

1. Put half of blueberry sauce in bottom of a 1-cup stemmed parfait glass or other small, clear decorative glass serving dish or bowl.

2. Spread half of yogurt over blueberries, then sprinkle all but 1 teaspoon of granola over yogurt. Top with remaining blueberry sauce, then spoon remaining yogurt over top. Garnish top with reserved 1 teaspoon granola.

Serve immediately, or cover and refrigerate parfait for up to 4 hours. (Granola will gradually lose its crunch with longer storage.)

Nutrition Facts

Serving Size 1 cup (209g)
Servings Per Container 1

Amount Per Serving

Calories 170   Calories from Fat 10

	% Daily Value*
Total Fat 1g	**2%**
Saturated Fat 0g	**0%**
Trans Fat 0g	
Cholesterol 5mg	**2%**
Sodium 120mg	**5%**
Total Carbohydrate 35g	**12%**
Dietary Fiber 3g	**12%**
Sugars 21g	
Protein 7g	

Mixed Berry Smoothie

This refreshing summer drink is ready when you are. Mixed frozen berries reduce the preparation time.

Makes 2 110-calorie servings, about 1 cup each.

1 cup mixed unsweetened frozen berries

1 cup reduced-fat plain, unsweetened Greek yogurt (made from 2-percent-fat milk)

1/2 cup cold water

2 Tbsp sugar substitute, or to taste

1. In a small microwave-safe bowl, microwave berries for 20 seconds to thaw slightly.

2. Combine berries, yogurt, water and sweetener in a blender container. Blend on cold-drink speed until uniform in texture, about 30 seconds. Serve at once.

Nutrition Facts

Serving Size 1 cup (244g)
Servings Per Container 2

Amount Per Serving

Calories 110   Calories from Fat 20

% Daily Value*

Total Fat 2.5g	4%
Saturated Fat 1.5g	8%
Trans Fat 0g	
Cholesterol 10mg	3%
Sodium 40mg	2%
Total Carbohydrate 15g	5%
Dietary Fiber 2g	8%
Sugars 10g	
Protein 10g	

Banana-Chocolate Breakfast Smoothie

This smoothie, pictured along with our Strawberry Lassi (see page 219), is a quick, easy, yet almost sumptuous way to kick off a busy diet day, although you can certainly prepare it for lunch or even supper if you wish. Simply toss all the ingredients in a food processor or blender, whir them together, and start sipping a surprisingly satisfying meal. Since the smoothie tastes chocolaty, it could even serve as a diet-day dessert.

To make sure the recipe fits into the diet-day calorie allowance, use a nonfat, reduced-calorie sweetened yogurt. Look for one with no more than 80 calories per 5.3-ounce cup; vanilla, coffee, cappuccino, and banana flavors all work well in this recipe. Also, if you're interested in getting the maximum protein for your smoothie money, choose a Greek-style yogurt.

Tip: If you omit the honey and use a sugar substitute, subtract 40 calories from the smoothie total.

Makes 1 170-calorie serving, about 1 1/4 cups.

1 5.3-oz carton "light and fit" or similar nonfat, reduced-calorie Greek-style vanilla-, coffee-, or banana-flavored yogurt

1 /2 small very ripe banana, cut into chunks

2 tsp unsweetened cocoa powder

2 tsp honey or sugar substitute of choice

Pinch of ground cardamom or ground cinnamon, optional

1 cup crushed ice

1. Combine yogurt, banana, cocoa powder, honey, cardamom (if using), and crushed ice in a food processor or blender container. Process or blend until completely smooth and well blended. Serve immediately.

Nutrition Facts

Serving Size 1 1/4 cups (326g)
Servings Per Container 1

Amount Per Serving

Calories 170   Calories from Fat 5

% Daily Value*

Total Fat 0.5g	**1%**
Saturated Fat 0g	**0%**
Trans Fat 0g	
Cholesterol 5mg	**2%**
Sodium 100mg	**4%**
Total Carbohydrate 37g	**12%**
Dietary Fiber 2g	**8%**
Sugars 25g	
Protein 6g	

Strawberry Lassi

Lassi, shown on the right in the photo, is a traditional Indian drink made with yogurt. This cool and refreshing version features strawberries. Garnish the tops with an extra sliced strawberry or two, if desired. Note: Our Banana-Chocolate Breakfast Smoothie is shown on the left in the photo.

Tip: You will need a little sugar substitute for this drink. Use your favorite, and add to taste. Or, if you prefer, sweeten with honey, and add 20 calories for each teaspoon used.

Makes 2 90-calorie servings, 1 cup each.

1 cup sliced strawberries

1 cup plain, unsweetened, reduced-fat yogurt

1/2 cup cold water

Sugar substitute to taste

1. Combine strawberries, yogurt, and water in a food processor or blender. Process or blend on medium speed until well combined and smooth.

2. Blend in a little sugar substitute, to taste.

Serve at once, topped with a sliced strawberry, if desired. Leftover lassi can be tightly covered and kept in refrigerator for 24 hours. Stir before serving.

Nutrition Facts

Serving Size 1 cup (317g)
Servings Per Container 2

Amount Per Serving

Calories 90   Calories from Fat 5

% Daily Value*

Total Fat 0g	0%
Saturated Fat 0g	0%
Trans Fat 0g	
Cholesterol 0mg	0%
Sodium 100mg	4%
Total Carbohydrate 15g	5%
Dietary Fiber 2g	8%
Sugars 13g	
Protein 8g	

Microwave "Grilled" Cheese Sandwich Snack

When we need a quick snack or just want a little something extra to go with a bowl of soup, this is one of the recipes we turn to. It's vaguely reminiscent of an open-faced grilled cheese sandwich, except it calls for a modest amount of shredded cheese and a reduced-calorie slice of bread. And, oh yes, the "grilling" is accomplished simply by zapping the sandwich in the microwave for about 30 seconds until the cheese melts and the bread is warm. Though the sandwich is light and the preparations simple, it makes a surprisingly satisfying snack.

Tip: To be sure your sandwich actually has the same number of calories as our version, choose a 2-percent-fat cheese and a "light" bread with only 40 calories per slice.

Tip: If you are gluten-free, substitute your favorite gluten-free bread. Since "light" (40 to 45 calories per slice) gluten-free versions are very hard to find, you'll likely need to do a little math and either reduce the amount of bread in the recipe or add the extra calories (over 40 a slice) contributed by the brand you substitute.

Makes 1 70-calorie serving, 1 slice of bread with cheese.

1 slice "light" multigrain or whole wheat bread

2 1/2 Tbsp shredded 2-percent-fat Cheddar, longhorn, or similar cheese

1. Put bread on a microwave-safe plate. Sprinkle cheese evenly over top.

2. Cover with a microwave-safe cover. Microwave on 50-percent power for 30 to 40 seconds until cheese just melts. Cut slice in half and serve.

Serve immediately as cheese will stiffen and bread will turn hard and dry if allowed to cool.

Nutrition Facts

Serving Size 1 slice (37g)
Servings Per Container 1

Amount Per Serving

Calories 70   Calories from Fat 15

	% Daily Value*
Total Fat 1.5g	**2%**
Saturated Fat 1g	**5%**
Trans Fat --g	
Cholesterol 5mg	**2%**
Sodium 190mg	**8%**
Total Carbohydrate 9g	**3%**
Dietary Fiber 1g	**4%**
Sugars 1g	
Protein 7g	

Microwave "Baked" Apples

If you choose the right varieties, microwave "baked" apples taste every bit as good as those readied in the oven. Actually, they come out more tender and succulent than traditionally-baked apples, and, of course, they cook in a fraction of the time. As a result, they are perfect when you're yearning for a quick, tasty snack or last-minute, diet-day dessert. We prepare them often.

After comparison-testing, we've discovered that some apple varieties "bake" much better in the microwave than others. The ones we like best are suggested below. All of them hold some shape, texture, and color, and taste pleasingly fruity. We don't recommend the readily-available Granny Smith because its skin turns olive drab and the flesh lacks sweetness. And we've found that the McIntosh splits apart and becomes soft and apple saucy.

Makes 2 100-calorie servings, 1 apple each.

2 small (2 3/4-inch) full-flavored fresh apples, such as Honeycrisp, Braeburn, Jonathan, or Golden Delicious

2 tsp packed light or dark brown sugar

2 generous pinches ground cinnamon or a few drops of vanilla

2 Tbsp apple juice

1. Using an apple corer (or paring knife if necessary), plunge down through apple centers, removing pithy cores and leaving a cylindrical opening running from top to base. Arrange apples upright in individual baking dishes or in a deep microwave-safe dish large enough to hold them. Don't crowd them, or their juices may bubble over dish sides during microwaving.

2. Spoon teaspoon of sugar into center cylinder of each apple. Put pinch of cinnamon or drops of vanilla into each. Drizzle half of juice over each apple. Cover dish(es) with a microwave cover.

3. Microwave apples, covered, on 100-percent power: At 5 minutes begin checking apples for doneness by piercing thickest part with a fork. Keep checking at 1-minute intervals until they are just tender; some varieties take much longer than others. Let apples stand a few minutes before serving. If apples were not readied in individual dishes, transfer them to individual bowls, and spoon cooking juices over them, dividing equally.

Serve immediately, or cover and refrigerate for up to 4 days.

Nutrition Facts

Serving Size 1 2 3/4-inch apple (169g)

Servings Per Container 2

Amount Per Serving

Calories 100   Calories from Fat 0

	% Daily Value*
Total Fat 0g	**0%**
Saturated Fat 0g	**0%**
Trans Fat 0g	
Cholesterol 0mg	**0%**
Sodium 0mg	**0%**
Total Carbohydrate 26g	**9%**
Dietary Fiber 4g	**16%**
Sugars 21g	
Protein 0g	

Frozen Banana Chocolate-Peanut Pops

These pops make a very convenient and decadent treat on a diet day. We keep them on hand in the freezer to satisfy occasional intense diet-day cravings for a sweet or dessert. Although we usually coat the pops with a combination of nuts and chocolate morsels, as you can see in the photograph, we sometimes keep the peanuts and chocolate separate and prepare two pops in each flavor. Take your choice.

Tip: Be sure to chop the peanuts and chocolate chips finely. They harden when frozen, and larger pieces become very difficult to chew.

Makes 4 90-calorie pops, half a banana each.

2 small (6-inch-long) fully-ripe bananas

1 1/2 Tbsp chopped dry-roasted, salted peanuts

1 1/2 Tbsp chopped, semisweet chocolate morsels

1. Peel bananas and remove any stringy bits. Cut bananas in half crosswise. Working from cut end and with one banana and one Popsicle stick at a time, carefully center stick and push it about 2 inches deep into banana halves.

2. If preparing combo pops, stir together peanuts and chocolate morsels; otherwise, keep them separate. Working at a cutting board or mat, spread out a quarter of combo coating or half of nuts or chocolate. Roll each pop back and forth until evenly coated, pressing down to embed coating.

3. Place pops in individual small, zip-top plastic bags, and seal airtight. Freeze until frozen, at least 2 hours or longer, for later use.

Frozen pops will keep for up to 3 weeks.

Nutrition Facts

Serving Size 1 popsicle (half a banana) (59g)
Servings Per Container 4

Amount Per Serving

Calories 90   Calories from Fat 30

% Daily Value*

Total Fat 3.5g	**5%**
Saturated Fat 1.5g	**8%**
Trans Fat 0g	
Cholesterol 0mg	**0%**
Sodium 10mg	**0%**
Total Carbohydrate 15g	**5%**
Dietary Fiber 2g	**8%**
Sugars 9g	
Protein 2g	

Pomegranate Pops

We find these pops a delightful sweet treat that not only provides a number of phytonutrients but some very satisfying munching. They are so easy to make and so convenient when we want a little nosh that we keep them in the freezer all the time. Double the recipe if you like.

Tip: Pomegranate juice is quite sweet without the addition of honey, so feel free to omit the honey from the recipe, if desired. In this case, each pop will have only 46 calories.

Makes 3 60-calorie servings, 1 pop each.

1 8-oz bottle pure pomegranate juice

2 tsp honey, optional

1. Thoroughly stir together pomegranate juice and honey in a 1-cup measure. Pour mixture into 3 3-ounce plastic cups, dividing equally.

2. Cover each cup with a small square of aluminum foil, smoothing it down over top. Cut a tiny slit into foil in center top of each cup. Slide Popsicle sticks into cups, adjusting so they stand upright.

3. Freeze cups, placed upright in freezer, for at least 3 to 4 hours or until frozen solid.

4. To unmold and store pops, run warm water over sides and bottom of a cup for 6 to 8 seconds. Squeeze on cup with one hand while pulling on stick with the other until pop slides out. Place each pop in a small plastic zip-top bag, and return to freezer.

Pops will keep, frozen and well wrapped, for up to 3 weeks.

Nutrition Facts

Serving Size 1 pop (80g)
Servings Per Container 3

Amount Per Serving

Calories 60   Calories from Fat 0

% Daily Value*

Total Fat 0g	**0%**
Saturated Fat 0g	**0%**
Trans Fat 0g	
Cholesterol 0mg	**0%**
Sodium 10mg	**0%**
Total Carbohydrate 14g	**5%**
Dietary Fiber 0g	**0%**
Sugars 14g	
Protein 0g	

AFTERWORD

Thank you for purchasing *The 2 Day a Week Diet Cookbook*. We hope you enjoyed using our recipes as much as we loved developing them.

If you liked the book and bought it from an online bookstore, do us a huge favor. Please go back to the bookstore and leave an honest review. Authors live and die by their reviews. The few extra seconds it takes are really appreciated. Thank you!

CONTACTS

Nancy and Ruth always love hearing from readers.

Contacting Nancy

You can contact Nancy through her Kitchenlane website: http://www.kitchenlane.com. Go to the **contact** tab in the navigation bar at the top to send her a message. Or click on **the 2 day a week diet cookbook** tab and leave her a comment about the book. Feel free to share any dieting success stories, ask for advice, or just say hello!

Sign up for Nancy's free newsletter: https://app.e2ma.net/app2/audience/signup/49815/7216/?v=a

Check out Nancy's videos on her YouTube channel: http://www.youtube.com/user/nancybaggettvideos/videos

Check out Nancy's Kitchenlane recipes, photos, and blog posts: http://www.kitchenlane.com

Connect with her on Facebook: https://www.facebook.com/pages/Nancy-Baggett-Bakes/156947697678428?ref=sgm

Contacting Ruth

You can contact Ruth at Rebecca@rebeccayork.com

Ruth's Web site is http://www.rebeccayork.com

Ruth's blog is http://www.rebeccayork.blogspot.com

On Twitter: @RebeccaYork43

On Facebook: https://www.facebook.com/RuthGlick

Some of Ruth's current fiction (writing as Rebecca York):

Dark Moon
Decorah Security Collection
At Risk
Nightfall
Bad Nights

AUTHOR BIOGRAPHIES

Nancy Baggett is the author of 16 cookbooks, including four that have garnered "best book" nominations from the International Association of Culinary Professionals and the James Beard Foundation. She is most well-known for her beautiful baking books but has been a contributing editor for *Eating Well* magazine for many years and has collaborated with Ruth Glick on a long list of healthy-eating and special-diet books. Together they created the recipes for the American Diabetes Association's *One-Pot Meals for People with Diabetes*; Prevention's *Healthy One-Dish Meals in Minutes*; Surrey's *Skinny Soups*; and Rodale's popular *100% Pleasure: The Low-Fat Cookbook for People Who Love to Eat.*

Their very first cookbook together, a Times Books title called *Don't Tell 'Em It's Good for 'Em*, won a "best healthy cooking book" nomination from the International Association of Culinary Professionals and was featured in *Family Circle*.

A frequent television and radio guest chef, Nancy is a long-time contributor to *The Washington Post* food section and has written recipes and stories for many other national publications including *Cooking Light, Vegetarian Times, Better Homes and Gardens, The Los Angeles Times,* and *Country Gardens Magazine*. She is also a food photographer-stylist and created all the enticing images in *The 2 Day a Week Diet Cookbook*. She follows the 2-day-a-week regimen using the recipes in the book and is down to her lowest weight in more than fifteen years! Visit her blog: http//www.kitchenlane.com

A New York Times and USA Today best-selling author, **Ruth Glick** is known for her more than 100 romance and romantic suspense novels, written as Rebecca York. In addition, she has authored fifteen previous cookbooks, many with Nancy Baggett. Because of Ruth's focus on healthy eating, her expertise is in writing low-fat cookbooks for such publishers as Times Books, Rodale, The American Diabetes Association, and Surrey Books. *100% Pleasure*, written with Nancy Baggett for Rodale, was named as one of the 12 best cookbooks of the year by USA Today. Her *Snack Munch Nibble Nosh Book* was a best-seller for the American Diabetes Association. She is also the author of *Fabulous Lo-Carb Cuisine*. Her food and nutrition articles and recipes have appeared in *Diabetes Forecast, Family Circle, Weight Watchers Magazine*, and *The Washington Post*.

After learning about the 2-day diet, designing some suitable recipes, and starting to lose weight, Ruth wanted to share her excitement about the eating plan. She teamed up with her longtime cookbook collaborator and friend, Nancy Baggett, who not only contributed recipes but took the stunning photographs for the book. At this writing, Ruth has lost sixteen pounds and looks forward to shedding more.

INDEX

CPSIA information can be obtained
at www.ICGtesting.com
Printed in the USA
LVOW05s2300150317

527399LV00050B/1198/P